"I love you, Me"

7 STEPS TO
TRANSFORMATIONAL SELF-LOVE

Tara Love Perry

I LOVE YOU, ME

7 Steps to Transformational Self-Love

By Tara Love Perry

First Edition January 2017 Transcendent Publishing

Address:
Transcendent Publishing
PO Box 66202
St. Pete Beach, FL 33736
www.TranscendentPublishing.com

Transcendent
Publishing

ISBN-10: 0-9982869-8-2

ISBN-13: 978-0-9982869-8-3

Printed in the United States of America.

With Love

For you; the one who looks for love; who wants to understand the true meaning of love; who wants to live completely liberated, in a space of love; fulfil your life and make a difference ~ this book is for you. I also wrote this especially for your children, those here now and those yet to come, so that together we could make this world a better, more loving place for them to grow up in.

I also dedicate this book to Phil, because I wanted most of all for you to love and forgive yourself. Instead I realised where I most needed to love and forgive myself.

Contents

In Gratitude

For all the teachers in my life, my parents and my siblings. I am grateful to have grown up in a community of people aspiring to realise Truth and attain inner peace.

I am supremely grateful to Prem Rawat, aka Maharaji, my spiritual master who never failed to remind me that what I am looking for is within me. It's a lifetime's journey to truly learn and understand this message.

I am supremely grateful for my children who consistently motivate me to be the best person I can be. They've taught me the art of forgiveness, compassion and unconditional love. Darshan and Sunny, you're the best!

I am grateful for my friends who watch me grow and encourage me to be all that I am. Thank you for allowing me to shine.

I am grateful for all my clients who trusted me to read their soul energy. Through you I learned and was guided by spirit. I am grateful for all my students who trusted me to teach them. As I taught you the more I discovered my own gifts. Thank you for trusting me.

I am grateful for the many people who encouraged me to write this book, who asked to have the principles in writing, who asked for my guidance. You gave me confidence. Thank you for believing in me.

I am grateful for the people who made this book tangible. I am so thankful that you helped me create my vision and make it available in the world, especially you Mum.

I am eternally grateful to Spirit, to the Life that breathes me; the ultimate teacher. Without you I wouldn't be having this experience of being me. I wouldn't exist. You constantly inspire me and urge me to co-create with you. I love being One with you, Life. Thank you for this opportunity.

And last but not least, I am super grateful to You. Thank you for being here, in this life, sharing this experience with me. Thank you for reading this book, for loving it, for sharing it, for wanting to help make it available in so many countries. Thank you for your feedback, for your stories and for your willingness to test these 7 steps. Thank you for choosing self-love and for making such a difference to your own life and to the world, for which you will mostly never know just how much you've contributed. I love you.

Preface

Why You're Here

Congratulations on picking up this book! It's no coincidence that you are now holding these pages in your hands. It's as if the Universe has guided you to this exact right spot, to deliver you the most powerful message. A message that will radically change your life. A message that can and will solve a great deal of your biggest problems. A message so profound that you've been waiting for forever, and now you're ready to hear.

Once you hear this message it's going to stay with you throughout the rest of your life. Once you understand the power of this message, you will want to share it far and wide. You'll tell it to your friends and family. You'll teach it to your children and your grandchildren. You'll want to share it with all those people in the world you care about, that you can influence, and those you want to help.

If you could solve the biggest problem in your life, WOULD YOU DO IT?

We all have the same problem. The problem is, that essentially, when it comes down to it, we all want to know how to be happy and free! We all want to be free of our problems and live the life we dream of living. There is one, simple ingredient that we can all add to our lives to make everything we want and need possible, to make everything come unstuck, that allows a bright new future to unfold, all pain to disappear and suffering end. Yes, really.

It's just that almost everybody misses it and virtually no-one knows how to do it yet. This is why it's so important that you're reading this book...

As you read, you'll have revelations about yourself and your life. You'll realise why things haven't worked out for you the way that you wanted or the way you planned. You'll understand why you've been struggling with the most fundamental issues in your life, such as what's going wrong in your relationships, why your health isn't up to par, why you don't have enough money, or why you're not feeling fulfilled at work. You'll have flashes of inspiration and wake up calls about what's been at the heart of every problem, fear and uncertainty. It's possible that you'll have a self realisation, finally seeing who you are, and what you are here to do, in this world. That's my wish for you; that's the possibility.

A 7 Step Feast

This message comes not in chapters, but in steps. Like a 7 Step dance, that once learned will always bring you joy. Or a 7 course meal that will perfectly satisfy you and never tire of feasting on. It's deliciously simple, easy to digest and gives you an abundance of goodness.

Imagine feeling more powerful, confident and valuable in life now because you have a formula to dissolve the blockages, pains and problems that have been holding you back. You now know how to clear the way so that you can move forward effortlessly and fearlessly. You need never feel lost, disconnected or alone again. You now have this new ability to liberate yourself in any situation, relationship or circumstance, so that you never feel helpless, abandoned or struggling again. Imagine you know exactly what to do to bring peace and clarity to your inner-conflict in any environment. You know exactly how to influence every aspect of your life, aligning yourself with your destiny and opening the doors to your fulfilment. Imagine that!

With <u>this</u> information, you can know who you are, where you've come from, where you're going and where you belong.

The answer you have in your hand, right now, has eluded most people throughout history. Relatively speaking there are only a handful of people on this planet who grasp the knowledge that's within these pages, and the power of what it can do. With the abundance of doctrines, philosophies and religions you would think we'd have the answers to freedom by now, and that we'd be happy. But we're not. Somehow we've missed something. Billions of kind, intelligent, aware and worthy people still suffer, despite having read the books, done the courses and got the information. So what are we missing?

There's only one vital thing needed to close the gap between the spiritual teachings and the day to day reality. Something that makes the divine and the human not so far apart. A real thing, that's easily tangible and attainable, without the need for sacrifice or endless reaching. And now you are here, with this opportunity of realisation and transformation at your fingertips. I believe that you are here for a reason. It must be your time to unlock this knowledge, set yourself free, and become who you came here to be. This is your wake up call. It's time for your world to change and open to a new perspective.

Are You Ready For That?

Despite this message being for everyone, not everyone is going to be ready for it. It is too simple and powerful. It will blow away familiar beliefs and concepts about who we think we are. Not everybody is ready for that level of change, despite being absolutely desperate and hungry for it.

Ironically this is the biggest paradox in history! It's been the biggest mystery to solve, and the hardest thing to grasp let alone attempt to *do*. I believe it's our greatest challenge as human beings to fully achieve it, and yet within the practice of it lies our path to enlightenment and self-mastery.

Here, in this book, lies the key to the solution to all of your life's problems. It is currently igniting a social revolution. The realisation and implementation of this message begins the awakening of our human evolution.

I believe the answer is Self-Love.

Beloved friend, it's my privilege and joy to share with you today the 7 steps of self-love that will be very different to anything you have experienced up until now, even if the idea isn't new to you. Would you be willing to allow me to lead you in the dance of Absolute Love; radical, deep, empowering Self-Love? Seven steps to the kind of Self-Love that will revolutionise your life, be a game-changer in your relationships with others, and evolve your consciousness to the next level, simultaneously.

I know! That's a big claim to make.

You might be wondering what kind of back-up I have to substantiate that?

Well, as you go through these pages you will see for yourself. Judge by your own experience. If you need convincing, ask your heart. If you feel a funny little tingling that this might be true, that you indeed hold this book as testimony of what **you secretly already know,** that you were drawn here for a reason, then would you be willing to trust your instincts and read on?

This is a message from your divinely intelligent self to your normal, every-day self, handed to you in a bunch of pages that I was tasked to write down for you. This message is not new information, it's as old as the hills and probably the Earth herself. Yet here it is, fresh and new, inviting you to the cutting edge of your awareness. Inviting you to step up, take the challenge and become the one who makes the difference to your own future, and create ripples that will affect the future of humanity.

You think I'm stretching it a bit too far?

Then start with knowing that you've picked up this book because you could do with loving yourself just that little bit more. And if you did love yourself that bit more, what might you attract into your life that you don't currently have? What might you give or allow yourself that you currently block or deny? What could you make possible that currently seems impossible?

Let's begin the journey. Thank you for being here.

I love you!

"The greatest secret of all is just love and serve yourself and others... and you've gotta take care of yourself first so you can be fulfilled, and once you're fulfilled your purpose really is loving and serving other people — it's why we're here."
— Marc Allen, author, president and publisher of New World Library

Tara Trilogy Part 1

"Your task is not to seek for love,
but merely to seek and find
all the barriers within yourself
that you have built against it."
—Rumi

I wanted the kind of love that's within me to be available on the outside too; For the heart of the world to match my own heart; For the love to be as visible, tangible and real as it is in me. It started when I was a child.

I was conceived in London in 1972 during the time when my parents were helping to create an ashram (an indian term for retreat or place of religious tuition and worship). I was raised in an urban community of devotees following the enlightened Master, Guru Maharaji as he was called then, now known as Prem Rawat.

My naming was blessed by his mother Mataji, and growing up I always wanted to go with my parents to Maharaji's speaking events. I felt truth in his presence and in his words even though I was too little to properly understand them. My entire childhood world was centred around the attainment and practise of inner-knowledge, perfect love and self-less devotion with weekly 'Satsang' meetings in our house. (Sanskrit word for the communal speaking and sharing of 'Truth')

I wanted to receive Maharaji's special meditation techniques when I was very young, but was told to wait. I asked again when I was nine years old and still I had to wait. Finally, I received the 'Knowledge' at the age of twenty-three, which I still sometimes practise.

I have a vivid memory that's shaped my life. I was four years old, staring up at my parent's faces from my sitting place on the floor experiencing a Light, let's call it Divinity, God or Love. It's all around me and within me but I can't see it anywhere else in my environment. I can't see that Golden Love anywhere as tangibly as is it in me. There seems to be a void between the light and the external world. As an adult I would call this experience that moment when one realises an apparent separation from Divinity, perfection, or God, in order to become human.

Earthly, human love looked and felt very different to the divine inner love; desperately lacking. My parents are smiling at me, and even though there's love between them, and love for me, something in their eyes tells another story. I see an attempt at love, they want it, they know about it, they believe in it, they feel the presence of Divine love within them too, but it's not always present. There's something not present in the day to day reality. The light stays inside, therefore making the world seem darker and more scary.

I see lies in the eyes of grown-ups that not even they know they're telling themselves. I see people lost. I see the grief in the layers of their irises, like veils blocking out the soul. They feel love in meditation, my devotee parents and their friends. They feel it in the company of the Guru, and then it feels wonderful. Love happens in their heart, in moments, but in the day-to-day reality so much of that peace, perfect love and light is missing. Outside of the inner sanctum of meditation and the self-less, spiritual landscape, I sensed a betrayal. I saw sadness. People in loss and lack. In the search for truth and peace I saw starvation of the soul and mixed messages flying everywhere. I sensed a fundamental lack of Love in this world and felt that I was not in the right place. Where's the love gone? Am I really being loved? Am I safe?

'Why isn't there love on the outside the way it is on the inside' is a question that tormented me for most of my life since having this experience. It made me sad. It made my little light dim.

Am I the only child to have felt like this? Was I the only one noticing the contrast?

No, I don't believe so. But it certainly felt like that for a very long time until I matured, healed, came out of my shell and connected with others.

My parents opened a healing centre when I was in my early teens, kick starting what has now become normal in today's society. They were among the first wave of 'alternative' therapists in the early 80's. I was fascinated by 'new-age' things and studied the healing qualities of crystals and essential oils. I played with the energy between my hands, I saw spirits, and taught myself the tarot. I was immensely sensitive, empathic and intuitive. But, for a long time it felt like a weird curse instead of something useful, and I was always being told that I was too sensitive, like it was a bad thing.

Despite being in this spiritual and healing environment, I became ill at fourteen, and for the next ten years my health slowly deteriorated until I was bed ridden with chronic fatigue and a host of related symptoms. In the end I was forced to heal myself and that's where my journey of self-love began. There is much more of this story to tell, some of it is scattered throughout this book. I think you'll relate to it and hopefully it'll serve you in a way that stories often do.

So I was stuck, really stuck. I felt powerless. I was helpless. I didn't feel safe in the world at all by then. I felt completely un-loved because no one was helping me or recognising my struggle and aloneness. I was full of 'poor me' and blame and pain towards 'Them' out there. Everything was overwhelming, so I created a safe little world of my own and floated around in a bubble. Parts of me were shut away in the cupboard of my heart for safety. Parts of me didn't even feel like they lived within my body, as if I was floating up there, out in the cosmos, searching for my home somewhere other than this world.

I amused myself with fantasies of love and daydreamed of my 'happily ever after', never actually finding it 'out there'. I idealised and closed my eyes and ears to the pain that was really happening inside of me. I got stoned. I drank. Then I meditated. I turned up the inner light to ignore the outer darkness of the world. I drowned out the chaos by chanting positive affirmations and devotional songs. I spent many years praying to be rescued, asking for redemption; as if I'd done something wrong to have deserved this human life and it was a punishment to be here.

Listening to Maharaji's talks were my respite and salvation. Faith in my inner feelings gave me something to hold onto. But nothing will arrest the test of time which will bring everything that was abandoned in the shadows creeping back for validation and acknowledgment. We cannot hide from parts of our own psyche or the truth in our heart.

The Power Of Validation

It was validation that began my journey to where I am now, so that I can sit here and write these words to you about how I healed all the undiscovered, lost or broken parts of my life, in my body, mind, heart and soul.

Someone saw me, saw the gift I was unconsciously hiding under my struggle, and encouraged me to bring it out into the world. He made me begin the journey to be my bigger self, My True self, by encouraging me to use my intuitive abilities.

It led me on a journey where I opened to my childhood sensitivities and began to use them. I was a single mother of two baby boys at the time. I was twenty nine years old and struggling to pay my rent and make ends meet. Having my intuitive gifts suddenly being validated was as if life had opened up a path for me. People immediately began coming to me for energy readings and paying me. With time and practice, ways of healing, clearing and mending the damage in the soul were also being revealed to me, and thankfully so. How twisted would it be if I could only read the pain and cause of people's suffering without being able to help them overcome it?

I crafted an art that I call Soul Reading, which is a bit like reading the Aura, or energy around a person, except it goes much deeper than that. I can read energy on many levels, ranging from your cellular memory and DNA coding to your emotional, mental, metaphysical and spiritual states of being.

I see 'past-lives' and a person's spiritual essence. I can see why they chose to be on this earth at this time and why they chose their parents. I see their untapped potential and pre-determined future, where they're headed and where they've become stuck or lost, and help to get them back on track.

I speak to spirits of people both living and passed. Through my connection to the light, spirit, God that I'd kept since childhood, I learned how to communicate with angels and tap into all manner of spiritual wisdom. I read from the 'Akashic Records', which is a Universal Library of all things that have ever happened ever, recorded as energy. Each Soul is like a room in that vast library, full of our soul stories and memories, all interconnected as part of the Whole.

I was in a school of Light, learning how to restore harmony. Ultimately, I learned that LOVE heals Everything. I learned that there are steps to love that must be taken for a soul to complete with its self, to be in peace and to heal. Love is what creates a soul. Love makes a soul thrive. Love makes a soul Evolve. Love is how life evolves itself.

And so I created the 'Live In Light Academy' in 2008 to teach 'Soul Reading' and psychic development, and my unique steps to self-love & healing that I've named "I love you, me" healing.

I've now worked internationally with thousands of people across nine countries and three continents teaching, healing and giving psychic and 'soul readings' in person, with many more online.

I find the patterns of human psychology, our origins and life purpose, fascinating. What makes us tick and what makes us stop ticking? What are our core needs, wants and desires? What motivates us? What is our end goal as a species? What influences us most, how and why? What is our true self and how do we be it?

I'm super passionate about the evolution of us human beings! I care that we seem to have been stuck in the same self-destructive patterns of behaviour and conditioning for aeons, and I know that it's time for us to break these habits and get free from these slavery bonds of our 'old paradigm' ways of thinking and behaving. I believe it's time for a new-earth. The ignorance of our history does not want to keep repeating itself. We have to 'grow up' now.

I am soul-driven in assisting people to become more self-empowered, on purpose in their lives, and able to achieve their heart and soul's calling. Life fulfilment matters. Self-realisation matters. Life wants this for you; for all of us.

Results

The results I get are deeply personal to those who have experienced a 1:1 Soul Reading/Healing session with me. My clients are met and touched in the deepest and most profound way, often more than they can put into words. All of them gush praise, astonishment and feelings of inner-peace. They feel lighter, renewed, transformed and free.

I have students and clients from war torn countries, who've been hostages, and victims of abuse and torture, who've experienced huge relief within literally minutes of working with "I love you, me" healing, the 7 steps to self-love. People report long-term pain and illnesses disappear, even cancer patients recovered whilst working with me. My clients who had lost all hope, lost their soul and even lost their minds have experienced huge transformation and relief, and then found their feet. Some people use "I love you, me" to heal their broken hearts and find the perfect love relationships. For others it has ended their eating disorders or helped them find their purpose and live it powerfully. For everyone, the result is a greater connection to their most authentic self. It feels like a home-coming. They finally feel loved, in both a human and divine way. You'll find stories of real people throughout this book.

This book is my offering, to lead you through the steps I learned and still practice every day. It'll be like putting you in the car, giving you the wheel, teaching you how to drive and then giving you the map. Now you are free, independent and capable of going anywhere in your life! I'll guide you how to steer yourself away from the cliff edge of whatever disaster or suffering you are currently facing. It'll teach you how to take the road less travelled in your life, and clear away the disarray, open up the way, and leave a legacy of love behind you. By love we ascend. By Love we become a True human being.

My search for love led me to find the love that I AM and bring it to the outside world. In love, duality and separation ends. In love, there is unity.

Let this book be your mentor and your guide. Let it be the voice of your best friend, holding your hand, telling you truths and supporting you to grow that bit more.

These 7 steps to self-love are a foundation for any other spiritual work or beliefs in your life and are intended to compliment your current practices. This book is how to get back in connection with you. It's about what you can achieve when you feel relieved of all the baggage and you can just be you. This is about being in Peace with you. And it all stems from having the willingness to just love your 'You'.

TARA LOVE PERRY

Introduction

Blueprints And Conditioning

Passing The Baton

When an issue is not healed and harmony is not found, it remains an open case, just like in a Court of Law. The file cannot be closed. The file waits for the next person to decide to pick it up and attempt to solve it.

Your parents for example, have issues in their relationship with themselves and with each other; Everyone does.

The issues that they cannot resolve internally and continue to fight about in their relationship are the very same issues that were passed onto you. You were next in line. You inherited the case because it needed to be solved. How many unresolved cases are there in your family affairs?

Just look at your Mum and Dad, then, look at their Mums and Dads. The open files are passed down the generations like an unwrapped present that nobody wants to open, own and deal with... or that they've given up on. The issues of the past become the present, i.e., they **are still happening now**, and will continue to happen in the future until somebody decides to become the super powered hero of a game-changer, employ their right to freedom and bring the conflict or trauma back into a state of harmony.

The moment you were imprinted with the 'destiny' of this task was your conception. Like passing the baton in a relay race at your school sports day, it is now **your** turn to pick up all the unresolved disharmonies of your ancestral past, and you were not even born yet! You are literally made from the 'stuff' of your parents and come from an infinite line of ancestors whose pasts were not all left in a clean and healthy state. There are memories in their souls that are not yet able to completely rest in peace.

Everything Is Vibration

When you gestated in the waters of your mother's womb, every little thought and feeling that she had, vibrated though her, and resonated deep into your tiny, watery, vulnerable growing body. The sound of her voice and the environment around her made vibrational ripples, impacting upon little you, all of it naturally imprinting your impressionable psyche. We see this when the ripples of a lake imprint its shoreline, or the ocean recreates its wavy pattern in the sand as the tide recedes. In this way, the water of your mother's womb, influenced by her inner state and outer environment, duplicates vibrational patterns onto your shore, the particles of your matter; i.e., your cells. Water has memory. It holds and stores vibrational patterns and resonances. Homeopathy and vibrational medicine are a testament to this. So too is the work of the late Dr. Masaru Emoto, author of "Hidden Messages in Water," which, along with his other books, beautifully illustrates my point.

"Existence is vibration...words themselves actually emit a unique vibration that the water is sensing...Water exposed to words, "Thank you" formed beautiful geometric crystals, no matter what the language. But water exposed to "you fool" and other degrading words resulted in obviously broken and deformed crystals."
—Dr. Masaru Emoto

Dr Emoto demonstrated how water 'receives' the words vibrationally, either in written form or the spoken word.In further studies he conducted, water seemingly received and responded to vibrations of prayer and intention sent 'telepathically' over great distance. If this is true, it goes to show how sensitive we are as beings who mostly consist of water. Scientific estimates are between 75-90%. Imagine being in the womb, a bubble of water, where your body is made mostly of water, with every vibrational activity around you resonating through the womb and into your cells. Then imagine how each water molecule in your body retains that memory. Water is in your blood, your bones, your cells. These vibrations are imprinted into your emotional body through water memory, into the physical particles of matter known as cellular memory and into your DNA structure.

Nature shows us again where this is true. Have you ever seen a fossil where a creature's body lay, leaving an imprint of its form in the rock? Even in the vast, dry bushland of Western Australia, I have seen where an ancient sea has left its mark; ripples carved into huge slabs of rock where water used to be. Emotional ripples imprint cells the way water ripples imprint solid matter.

Crystals and gem stones store vibrations too. In fact, everything on this planet is some form of vibration, either appearing as a solid, liquid, gas or ether. When we look at our physical body in detail, down to the cells, we can see that they too are vibration in form, and consequently influenced by the other vibrational conditions that they originate from and those that surround it. In other words, your mother's cells are replicated to create yours, with your father's DNA codes injected into the formula. Then your cells are shaped by the 'weather' of external conditions in the womb environment, which is influenced by the relationships, family situations, social and cultural conditions that shaped your mothers experience during her pregnancy with you.

Next you were born, and as you ventured through the passage of the birth canal, you were incarnated and initiated and sealed into your unique 'blueprint' for this life. This blue-print holds the conditions of your ancestral inheritance, conception and gestation. These are challenges for you to meet and overcome, like finding boobie-traps along a treasure trail.

Within each challenge lies a hidden gift, a clue to your destiny! More on that later... back to baby you.

You were born! What did the world look like? What was your first impression? We all know the importance of first impressions - They impact us immensely. Who was there and what were their vibrations like? Happy? Positive? Welcoming? Or were they sour, scared, knocked out on drugs and painkillers, or just absent?

Every little first impression counts. It lets us know if we're in the right place or the wrong place. Did we land OK? Do we belong? Are we wanted here? We pick these things up instantly and it registers.

When you're a foetus or an infant you are not able to tell the difference between your body and your mothers'. You recognise yourself as part of her identity until you are about 3 years of age, so your mother's experience becomes largely what you believe yourself to be. You are consistently exposed to her thought environment. Her mind-set becomes your own.

Imagine that your foetal or infant brain is made of soft, impressionable clay. Then imagine your mother pushing her hand into the left side of your mind and leaving a deep hand-print, but you remain completely innocent and unaware of this. As you grow up your mind hardens, your thinking becomes more rigid like hardened clay. Your mother inadvertently left her mark which dominates the left hemisphere of your psyche, which just happens to be where your ego or self-identity chip is rooted. (Imagine a data stick programmed to inform the rest of the organism, i.e. you, that you are a singular, separate being, and it's stuck into the top, middle, left side of your brain.) Your own soul signature tries to establish itself within your psyche too, so that you have mental conception of who you are as a unique individual, with a right to exist separately from your mother. But the mother imprint is indelible, like the wave pattern imprinted on the rock, and all too often it over-powers our small child mind, over-riding our own identity chip. It's as if we can't get our mother's thinking out of our head. Like Siamese twins joined in the mind, you share the same thought processes and self-identity beliefs. Your brain either attempts to work around this, tries to eliminate it, or concedes to it. And throughout our formative years we're exposed to her voice and many more of her emotions and vibrational patterns.

Even as an adult it is hard to make a separation and discern the difference between whose pattern is whose? Is it your own thinking or your mother's?

It is therefore vital to our own self-identity, and emotional and mental health that we do this psychological separation from our mother in a healthy and supportive way as we grow to adulthood, hopefully resolving conflicts and evolving beliefs peacefully together. Rituals and rites of passage ceremonies during puberty have historically been done for this purpose, but for most people this doesn't happen. We're often somewhat enslaved, stuck with our inherited conditioning as if we have someone else's software governing our brain, despite not agreeing with it or particularly relating to it as our 'Self'.

It can spur us on to go looking for our 'Self'.

Conditioning also comes from your father. His subconscious and unconscious belief system hand-print is all over your right brain. All of his conditioned thinking about life, God, the universe and everything, transferred to your mind. It has an influence and can interrupt your own original, creative thinking. You take it as your mind and respond to it personally. We don't realise that what he thinks about himself is what we think he thinks about us. That's why people all too often think that their father doesn't really love them or have a high value of them because in fact he has a low value of himself. But he contracted this mind-set from his father, and so on.

Remember, that these beliefs aren't always on the surface and readily perceivable - They are the deep inner-workings of a very complex psyche which has developed over countless millions of years of humanity. As flowers in a garden become cross pollenated, either by design, or by so-called 'accident'; whatever you want to believe, we could easily have been cross-contaminated with other species within this universe. I have certainly seen non-human DNA attached to the regular human DNA, it's more common than you would think. And since everything that each one of us personally and collectively experiences is recorded on every level of existence as a vibration, as I explained earlier with water and solid matter, we must expand that awareness to include mental and etheric imprinting too.

Our thoughts impact our reality. Our spiritual beliefs and ethereal experiences impact our reality. The spirits of your passed over loved ones and ancestors affect your reality, but many people don't realise this. Think of people who feel guided or protected by angels, or who hear the voice of their deceased grandmother or grandfather speaking to them, either in prayer or in dreams. How many people believe they hear the voice of 'God' speaking to them, telling them what to do? If we are only conscious of a maximum of 10% of our mind, how much do we not yet know that we don't even know? What else exists beyond the 10%?

A new piece of understanding creates a new wave in the pattern. But all too often our minds look like an old vinyl record with deep cut grooves that we replay again and again and again, and we can't cut a new song into an old record. Our normal daily thinking becomes stuck in the well-worn grooves and we can't see the way out, even though there is an infinite horizon of new possibility in every direction, just above the groove. We need to change the record.

As far as your father's creative thinking and spiritual quest to know himself has got, this you will inherit. And of course what he thinks he sometimes speaks of; not always directly, but his deep-seated beliefs do escape through his everyday language and impact you, again. It ingrains the genetic conditioning further.

As a foetus we are alchemically primed to recognise the father's voice and tone, and respond. His tone has maximum effect and influences the development of the foetus more than any other, resonating into the womb waters. His sperm contains his whole genetic blue print; a map of his entire belief system (conscious and unconscious) along with the emotional and spiritual conditioning and DNA encoding that he's inadvertently inherited from *his* predecessors, which then directly seeds the blueprint of *your* Being.

His is the seed from which the tree of You grows. Your mother is your soil. Imagine all of the ingredients that consist of your Dad, his inner most theories, beliefs, principles, guilt, shame, fears and phobias. He was made of a concentrated droplet of his father, and now he has condensed all that he is and flavoured your self-identity with just one-drop; the stock of his breeding.

Your procreation was a duplication of your parents physiological and psychological conditions, therefore transference of these conditions continues as the next child in the lineage is born; your child.

SEED + ENVIRONMENT = BABY

The Seed And The Soil

As we know, food grown from organic seeds and organic soil are the preferred choice these days, but the cost is high. It's a tall order in our world today to have a high standard of purity and good health. Our soils are depleted of nutrients, our waters are polluted, our air is toxic and the spiritual highways bombarded and bombed, hijacked and pillaged by terrorists of religion, dogma and power. There are very few safe environments anywhere. Even the seeds of our food crops are poisoned by pesticides, and often genetically modified so as to inhibit the plant's natural re-production system, making certain corporations vastly more profitable and able to dominate and control our food industry.

Is it any wonder that people have become infertile, unable to naturally reproduce like the genetically engineered seeds? Women are becoming more barren and unable to nutritionally and emotionally support a precious, pure new life, perhaps like the ecosystem of the planet? And men's seeds are becoming tainted with preservatives, organophosphates, frustration, grief and despair at their apparent lack of power to make a significant change in the world, in the face of such terrorism against our natural laws. The transference of poisons into our ecosystems needs to stop and be restored, just like the blue-print of our human conditioning needs to be wiped clean and healed. Don't we all want real, uncontaminated food? Don't we all want the baton to stop being passed to the next generation, as it was to us?

Dancing To The Tune Of Our Own Flute

Aside from all this conditioning, as a new born baby you were pure and innocent. Like pure distilled water, you attracted and absorbed toxins from your environment by default, in order to help purify your surroundings.

Consider your origins and immediate surroundings when you were tiny.

Now, think about your vibrational signature as being harmonic, perfect and crystalline. The distinction between your vibration and the vibrational signature of those around you was an enormous contrast for you to integrate with. By your very nature of purity, it was pre-determined that the only way for you to belong, or fit into your environment was to **share the disharmony** by assuming the burdens and heaviness in the atmosphere around you.

In other words, you didn't vibrationally match your environment. Therefore, you instinctually try to raise the local vibration to meet your own by making others happy, just so that **you** can be happy. Sometimes this works. Most often it's futile and we feel as if we have failed. Grown-up business is heavy for us to lift. You absorb pain, negativity or feelings of emptiness like a sponge, in an attempt to clean up the space, so it feels better for you to exist in. In an effort to create harmony, love and belonging, you instinctually become enough like those around you to just fit in and survive.

This is what I notice. All children are highly sensitive. They perceive and are empathic to SO much more than adults give them credit for. As children, we might not have cognitively understood the complex dynamics of relationships or situations happening around us, but we could **feel** it. We knew when something wasn't right. We felt a dissonance, an in-congruency, a distortion in the field.

We children felt the unspoken feelings in the room, the tensions between people, the tones of voice, the furtive looks. Do you remember? We breathed in that atmosphere. Like inhaling invisible smoke in a room we inhaled the thoughts and feelings. We had to swallow down the words that were flying around us, both spoken and unspoken. It all had an impact and landed somewhere inside us.

Children's perceptions tend to go unrecognised and unvalidated, which means they feel alone with it all. Commonly this renders a child to feel like they don't belong, that they're wrong or they're weird, despite the best parenting efforts.

Imagine a symphony all playing off-key, out of tune and in chaos. You arrive with your flute and start playing a beautiful, sweet melody. How long would you feel comfortable in such an environment? How long could you maintain your harmony and melody? You begin to question yourself. You begin to think that the contrast you experience between them and you means that you are in the wrong. You are the fault. Your mental and emotional health begins to hang in the balance as you try to figure this out without proper guidance and validation. When our environment, i.e., family, society, world etc, is unsympathetic to our authentic, natural and true state of being, (and we have no apparent choice **but** to be here because we've been born), we begin to 'autopilot,' functioning mostly in coping mechanisms whilst largely disregarding our innate inner knowing.

We perceive that we have to compromise who we are to survive. We stop playing our own tune and become discordant like those around us.

Consequently our sensitivity, openness, innocence, trust and willingness to play along with life becomes extremely compromised in such situations.

The intuitive senses become less open, less astute and less responsive. We begin to shut down, become detached, close up, feel fear and not know why.

Emotions and thoughts that stem from this fear are too much to handle as a child. They overwhelm us. At this point we must cast away and drift off into a 'world of our own' to disconnect from the harshness of the 'normal' reality around us. Perhaps we go and find a different orchestra, one that plays our kind of harmony, but mostly we find ourselves chronically alone and displaced.

Lack of validation and engagement with our sensitive nature and our childhood feelings creates life-long disabilities. We grow up with holes in us. We begin 'The Search' to fill those holes. We have to discover ways to cope, and ways to survive as best we can. We search for meaning, and connection and love. We search to find out who we are.

Undoubtedly your parents did their best. They were good as they could be, as their era, history, culture and conditioning allowed them. They followed what they thought was the best solution for a successful and prosperous life and a happy family, whether it was chasing money or power, abiding by religions, or being moulded by moralistic materials of another nature. They loved as they were taught to love, and added their own versions on top. Each generation has tried to escape some of the emotional entrapment and mental slavery of their predecessors. We try to change the past, put it behind us and move forward. Ironically, it's to our own detriment. We cannot escape the past. Time does not heal, it merely buries. So much has gone unnoticed. So much has been swept by time under the carpet of our sub-conscious memory cover-up.

Millions of therapists worldwide would agree that almost all of our adult complaints and problems started in childhood. The past comes back to bite us not because of Karma or some kind of punishment or atonement from God. I don't believe that, although I used to. But rather because ghosts will rise from a grave where the person was not buried with peace in his soul. What lies in the foundations will seep up through the framework of our new, positive self-build lives.

In trying to escape the past we separate. We cut off. We bury. We hide. If something doesn't work for us, we get worked up, get justified, try to work it out, or we leave. We close doors, close our hearts, close our minds and slowly but surely, shut down. Then we try to control the future.

Many of us have had to move away from uncomfortable or intolerable situations that we were either born into or had to suffer at some point in our lives. Like orphans or refugees we had to flee from the homeland to find safety.

We humans scatter ourselves like leaves to the wind, torn apart by life experiences, unable to come to terms with or properly heal what's happened to us. To survive another day and preserve our sanity, we create a paradigm separation between the trauma and our self-identity. Our souls become fragmented in torment and our minds split in non-equatable realities. We become numb to our instinctive emotions and stop relating to our 'Self' in our true nature. causing us to lose our innate identity, to lose our thread, and lose our rag. As a result we then have difficulty relating to others in a transparent, intimate and un-fearing way.

You're Not Alone

I'm not telling you all this to scare you. But, imagine Ten million other people reading this book, feeling the same or similar to you. This information relates to everyone on a very deep level. You probably thought it was just you. Perhaps you didn't know all that stuff about gestation, ripples and conditioning, you just know that you don't feel like yourself, and often feel lost, disillusioned and freaked out by the world? I give you this information as a lens to look through, so you can see that every person on this planet has come through the same door, a similar birth to you, and they too can feel like an alien on their home planet!

We all come with conditioning, and it's not all your fault. But it's not "all their fault" either. Blue-prints of our soul journey are invisible to most people, but that doesn't mean we don't see the effects of it, all around us. We can clearly see how conditioned humanity has become; saturated, stained and distorted by it. We clearly see that something big is needed. A simple medicine that everybody can swallow that isn't owned by some corporation with a control agenda. We need something real and true.

And that my friend is why you are here. Bear this conditioning in mind as you traverse the 7 steps. Somewhere between taking things too personally and feeling overburdened and in pain with the severity of it, there's a balance. Understand that it's a collective issue that every human being faces, without dismissing your own personal responsibility to heal it. Between the two we can find enlightenment and inner peace.

"Out beyond ideas of wrongdoing
and rightdoing there is a field.
I'll meet you there.
When the soul lies down in that grass
the world is too full to talk about."
—Rumi

Gold Linings

The Golden Buddha

In the time of the Sukhothai Dynasty in Thailand during the 13th-14th centuries, a huge Buddha was made. It was later moved to the beautiful ancient city of Ayutthaya in 1403. Then the Burmese invaded Thailand in 1767, destroying the Ayutthaya Kingdom. The statue, seemingly made of Stucco, a kind of plaster cement, painted and inlaid with bits of coloured glass, was overlooked and remained amongst the ruins of the city unnoticed for 24 years. In 1801, Thai king Buddha Yoda Chulaloke (Rama I) ordered that the various Buddha images from the ruined temples around the country should be brought back to the newly established capital city of Bangkok.

The Buddha was moved a number of times, left in temples of disrepair, and even under a simple tin roof for 20 years when there was no temple large enough to house it. Until finally in 1954, a new temple was built to house the enormous statue.

In the move to its new location on 25 May 1955, during the final attempt to lift the statue from its pedestal, the ropes broke, and the statue fell hard on the ground. At that moment, some of the plaster chipped away. The story goes that one of the monks took a torch to inspect the damage, and upon shining the light into the cracked plaster, he noticed gold glinting from within it. A full inspection was made and the plaster was carefully removed to reveal that in fact the Buddha was made entirely of gold! It had been covered in plaster to protect it from being stolen by the invaders almost 200 years previously.

It was found that the gold statue, approximately 3.9 meters high and 3.1 meters from knee to knee, actually consisted of nine parts that fit smoothly together. A key was also found encased in plaster at its base, which can be used to disassemble the statue, allowing for easier transportation.

At US$1,400 per troy ounce, the gold in the statue (18 karat) is estimated to be worth 250 million dollars. The body of the statue is 40% pure, the volume from the chin to the forehead is 80% pure, and the hair and the topknot, weighing 45 kg, are 99% pure gold.

The true nature of the Buddha is pure gold, yet was hidden from plain sight beneath a thick layer of cement to protect its value until such time as deemed safe for its real identity to be revealed. This, my friend, is how it is with you. Self-love is the key that fits all the pieces of your nature together.

The Golden Buddha at Wat Traimit

Golden Linings

As with everything in Life, the cycle must be completed. Life will bring up everything that it needs to in order to grab our attention and pull us back to our origins. We must return 'home' to confront the dissonance that interrupted our harmony. It is essential for our healing.

What does that mean?

Whatever you fled from will re-surface, like a ghost that won't leave you alone. The file must be closed. The baton must not to be passed to the next child in your family. You cannot run from the truth or your shadow. You may employ huge amounts of resistance and live in self-protective denial, but it is the default mechanism, the law of the universe, for the beginning to one day meet the end. This is the cycle. This is where you come in.

Being human, with our currently limited foresight and limited understanding, we kick and scream and shout and cry ourselves to exhaustion in the struggle to come to terms with this kind of reconciliation. We would rather believe against all sense, that 'Life' is against us. We can't see above the groove.

We say things like: "Oh, that's just life" or "Life is hard" or "It's not my responsibility" or "I'm leaving" or "I can't **cope** anymore."

Some continue fighting to the death.

When we fight with life, we cannot win. We can resist the intelligence of life to remain in integrity with itself, but life cannot exist if it is not in cohesion with that which it supports. Life has an almighty and powerful will to get you to come back into synch with the natural law and divine order of things, so as to fulfil itself! Like the tide on the ebb, drawing back to itself, life will draw you towards your redemption; a saving grace instructed to return you to wholeness.

In other words, the beginning must meet the end. For some, this is an exit. They give up, or give in, and leave this body.

Never Abandoned

Life will never give up on us, but, we can give up on it, and let go, unable or unwilling to continue. We largely believe that we are powerless to change our own circumstance or the world around us, and powerless to make others do our bidding or wishful thinking. So we go round and round on the merry-go-round of carnation. Death is no real way out, just a resting spot, a costume change. When we realise this; that we've got very stuck in a loop, like a needle in a record, caught in the karmic hamster wheel of history repeating itself over and over, wouldn't it be useful to get off that wheel and choose a different experience now?

Let's untangle you from the pain and get free of the wheel now. Let's remove the stucco and reveal the golden nature of who you are. I'm going to show you the steps that any child can do and yet has brought the most stubborn, grown man to his knees to weep in relief. It will turn you on and tune you in! Alight your senses and tickle your fancy! It Works. On. Everything

I'm excited! Let's dive into the first of the 7 steps of Self-Love.

LOVING MYSELF ENOUGH
TO CONNECT WITH ME

'Hello Breath'

What comes and goes forever, unseen and unheard, giving you everything you have and asking nothing in return, yet silently demanding our full attention if we are to be happy, healthy and fulfilled, as if our very lives depend on it?

The very first step to understanding anything at all about ourselves, life and love is something so simple that we mostly take it for granted. We do it constantly, yet not very well considering that we've been doing it all our lives. Many, if not most people forget that it is even happening; Our Breath.

From nobody knows where, and returning to God-only-knows, a breath humbly and elegantly enters this temple of our mortal matter and brings it to life. On a physical level the automated action of the lungs inhaling oxygen, naturally present as air, feeds the heart and organs of the body the way steam runs an engine, but that's not all.

If we think about it, it's not only humans that breathe. All life on this planet respires in some way. We turn the soil to oxygenate it, preparing it to make our flowers and vegetables grow. Without oxygen water becomes a putrid, gloopy, foul smelling substance that is unsafe to drink and ceases to support life. It's in common with all other creatures; birds, mammals, fish and insects alike. We are all stroked into life by the power of breath. It's been happening on this planet for billions of years, with an estimated 6 or 7 million years of human existence. As long as there is breath, there is hope, renewal, a chance for life. When the breath stops and leaves on the ex-hale, so too does the force that animates. Without breath our bodies decompose and rot back to our original state; mud. Blending our elements with those of the Earth; ashes to ashes, dust to dust. And still the mud breathes. Life still happens.

It stands to reason that perhaps breath holds the Key to the Bigger Picture of existence? Perhaps there's a bit more to it than we realise? What does the 'Force That Breathes Us' know that we do not? Breath is the kiss of life, so why do we not receive it's unconditionally loving embrace anywhere near as much as we could? Could we kiss Life back (metaphorically) and really let the love flow? Could Life be offering us a relationship that we are resistant to, even ignorant of, getting into? It could save our lives...

Life Saved You The Moment You Were Born

From the moment we were born it blessed and held us. As babies we were soft, humble, able to receive its gift without resistance, control or ego. We trusted implicitly because that was all that was required of us.

It's the very first action we took; we received the breath. We received life exactly as it is.

Something divine filled that little body with light and purity, and it radiated out like love, so untainted, so holy that all wanted to be near us. Could that same light and purity still be coming to us every day, knocking at a door that we've closed against it? Could life's kiss be the very essence of unconditional love?

We have forgotten to trust, forgotten to soften, forgotten to receive, forgotten that we are being breathed; that life is doing us and that we are not doing IT. We fall asleep and lie there dreaming, thinking we are awake, and still the breath gently keeps us.

When I'm asleep I'm not aware of my breath. I'm not aware of what is real and what isn't. I'm in a world of my subconscious mind, even if I become awake within the dream as Lucid Dreamers do, I am still living a virtual life that seems real, until I actually wake up. My breath lets me know that I'm awake, I yawn and take in gulps of oxygen, stimulating my body and sensory motors into action. If I'm not aware of my breath as I live out my day, am I truly awake, or still dreaming?

Awaken

I believe consciousness starts with Breath. If we have not yet become conscious of the very spirit and super-substance which permits our moment by moment presence in this body and on this earth, are we are not missing something? And, I'm not talking about counting breaths, like counting our blessings or counting sheep, and I'm not talking about regulating, manipulating or controlling the breath to achieve specific states of mind either.

Like listening to the sound of the wind through the trees with an innocent ear, or watching the waves on the ocean with eyes of wonder, or touching the soft petals of a blossomed rose with the curiosity of a child. Have we heard and seen and felt the breath like this?

Have we embraced its light like the humble sunflower or the tiny buttercup, who's face never leaves the sun's blaze? Have we drunk deeply of its kindness and generosity as it begs us to take our fill again, and again? Have we noticed it's sweet caresses tumble within us like a soft, cascading waterfall, to be bathed, refreshed, enlivened down into the deadest, darkest most forgotten places within us?

We wonder why things aren't going our way,
When it's we who aren't going the way of Life.

We think we've got a grip on things, that we have a handle on life, that we know the way - until we're lost again, fighting for our lives, feeling out of control and exhausted from so much holding on.

In defence and self-protection we bury in deeper, maximising our border patrol. The nervous system goes on high alert, ever watchful, vigilant and anxious for any signs of attack. We clamp the throat to guard the vault of aged and well-preserved feelings, so that the lightest breeze of incoming breath does not disturb the sediment of deep down fear. Mostly living only in our mind and thoughts, we sift, sort, strategise and search, trapped in the penthouse office of our head instead of occupying all floors of this mortal abode.

Could we sacrifice our resistance and cravings for control to something greater and wiser than ourselves? Could we melt in relief at not having to be the 'grown up' for once, and having it all sorted? Could our body yield to the pleasure of our every molecule sprung open like an unfurling baby fern, and the chatter of the mind disabled by the soothing nectar of letting go? When did we last come home, drunk in-love, giddy with joy, simply soaking in the deliciousness of every morsel of every minute of being given to, so simply, so unconditionally? When?

The breath is the most trustable, tangible thing that we have to hold onto in our daily life. It is literally our life-line. It's a rope that's thrown to us, but frequently leave hanging in the air un-grasped.

It has been with us since the first moment we were born and will be with us until the very last moment, at our apparent 'death'. It is as continuous as the shore-lapping waves, persisting night and day without our attention or effort. It is the pillar of strength as it rises and falls within us, more powerful than we are to resist it. It is the basis of our existence and the parental, ever present force of love, whether we allow ourselves to fully receive it or not.

Our breath is also an incredible tool, a vehicle in which to travel, requiring our conscious attention. We need to stay with it and *let it move us*, a bit like staying in your car when you're on a road trip. I liken the breath to the glass elevator in "Charlie and the Chocolate Factory" by Roald Dahl, because it can take you anywhere when you stay inside it.

The act of breathing is essentially receiving and releasing 'Prana', or the Universal energy. Both of these actions are effortless, natural and automatic in a healthy body. Yet, for most of us, we no more allow the reality and full potential of breath than we engage with the consciousness that it takes to truly receive it. To place consciousness on the Breath as it is enters and releases the body elicits a more conscious awakening generally, but this is just the beginning. The consciousness of your Breath will open all the doors within, take you places, throw on light switches and reveal the truth in you like nothing else. Breath's omnipresence shows where you're at and where you've been, and where you're going. Like a guide it will lead you, if you'll hold the torch of awareness, keep up with it and follow.

"Energy flows where attention goes."
—3rd Huna Principle of Life

Breath will awaken you to your Inner-senses and activate powers in you that you didn't even know you had. It's your personal magic genie to polish and make all your wishes come true. Breath will clean you, heal you and teach you. Breath will also keep delivering, just as it has done all your life. It's been there since the beginning and it'll be there until the end. It won't abandon you. It won't let you down, it's the real thing. It's the best friend a man, or woman can have. If only we would notice and engage with it. Hands up who wants a relationship with someone like this?

Bridge To Human Existence

This breath is the bridge between heaven and earth, between spirit and matter, our mother and our father. Your body is the flute for your eternal spirit's amusement; a dancing reed blown in the sacred breeze. It makes a bond of marriage for better and for worse between our immortal soul and our mortal body. So, until death do us part, can we love, honour and obey the force that unites all things? Could you open and receive, and be the gateway through which your spiritual purity descends to fill this worldly body with the light and intelligence of Life itself, the creative force that you are?

Do This Now

1. Notice how you're breathing. Is it deep or shallow?

2. Now take a deep breath. How does your throat feel, your chest, your tummy. Is it open or tight?

3. Notice what you might be holding in, or blocking out by how you receive and release your breath. Is it soft and easy, or are you controlling, restricting or forcing the natural flow? Do you let your breath reach down into your heart, or your tummy? Can you connect to the feelings and emotions inside you?

4. Notice if you really trust your breath to keep coming and giving to you?

5. Notice if you deep down trust in the natural flow of Life coming and giving to you?

Always An Open Door

Ideals and ideas of life are wonderful! We love them. However, they can prevent us from experiencing what's right in front of our noses because our attention is elsewhere. We can miss what life is offering us. We would be blind to it because we are not in the right place to receive it. Yet life is always holding an open door, waiting for you to experience its true nature. Will you go through? I'm going to share with you the first technique. I invite you to come open, and just for a while leave your clever mind at the door.

The "Breathe & Receive" Basic Practise

As if with the eyes and wonder of a child, watch how your body receives the breath. Notice the chest, abdomen, lungs and diaphragm moving as the air enters you. Notice this as 'the mechanics of breath'. Just notice them, allowing yourself to witness the mechanism of breath without control or judgment.

Gradually, graciously, allow yourself to soften and relax, letting your body become heavy. Continue to watch as the breath moves your body, giving itself inwardly and down. Notice what happens to your body, how it recedes, accepts and allows the fluid motion of the breath within you.

As you soften and become heavy, notice that the breath still continues to lift you and rock you in its rhythm. Completely let go and surrender to this rhythm and notice how it makes you feel to do so. Move with it in stillness, as it rocks you like a cradle.

You are completely held by this breath like a babe in arms. Remember that it is not you who is 'doing' the breathing but Life that is breathing you.

Surrender all control, if you can. Every thought, emotion or physical disturbance hand over to the breath. Give over everything as it comes to you, all tension and resistance. You may even like to imagine a tiny, mini little 'you' flopped on top this breath, gently rising and falling like an invisible elevator, up and down within the core of your body.

Notice now the very 'Essence of breath,' the core feeling of it, as you slip into the spaciousness within yourself, so graceful, silky smooth and effortless. There is nothing to do except feel. Breathe and receive. Breathe in what you feel. Notice how you feel.

So, staying with your breath as *it* moves **you** in a surrendered place, allow your mouth to drop open. Allow your jaw to completely relax and hang if need be. (You may like to stretch out your mouth and jaw a little to let it become loose) Let your throat soften completely, as it was when you were a newborn baby. (Both your unconscious mind and your body remember how that was)

Allow the breath to enter through the mouth and trickle down your throat like the river of life itself. Let the softening spread down through the core of your body, through your chest, heart, abdomen, stomach, lower belly (womb if you have one), down to the sacral area between your hips, and finally right down to the sitting place, your base.

Notice when your body is relaxed, yielded and passive that your breath can now enter you more easily. You are no longer trying, but ready for receiving. Receiving is a choice. It is not forced upon you. Would you like to receive more from life?

Surrender more. Open and receive unconditionally as the breath is given to you. Let all control melt away and feel the power of life that delivers you into existence. Lap it up. Drink it in. Stay present. Feel.

Let the breath now move into every cell of your body. Focus on your physical substance; the putty, the matter from which you are made. Notice how the breath brings the life force that glues your particles together; how you would simply dismantle and dissolve without it.

Notice the places in your body where you need to receive more energy, more power, more oxygen, more life force.

Open the doors inside every part of you where the doors are tight shut. Where you have never been, or looked, or breathed. Do it with total surrender and an open soft, baby mouth.

Receive the breath. Now close your eyes and continue to "Breathe and Receive," and feel.

The Master And The Student

Were you watching your breath move you from the safety of your control-tower head, or was your awareness moved? Did you allow your consciousness to travel, to enter the body's opening doors, to walk through in faith, following in the footsteps of your breath? Did you discover the rest of you?

If you notice the direction of your breath, of Life; it goes **within** you. It wants to go deep. When your body is soft, relaxed and trusting like a baby, it slides in effortlessly to **fill** you. Its directive, need and desire is to fully fill you so that you are not left empty, needing or lacking. It wants to serve you, not fight with you to get in and be received!

> *"How many times have you sat in a room and said,*
> *"God, if you're real, I want to see you"?*
> *And God came as the breath and blessed you.*
> *That is the truest blessing of all."*
> — *Prem Rawat*

The breath spoon-feeds you as much as you will accept. Its nature is to Give. And when you are done and have taken your sip, life releases you, allowing you to give back what no longer serves you on the out breath, unobtrusively, gently, no drama. It releases you softly, preparing you to receive again. Like a loving parent, it is always there, giving, guiding and holding you, encouraging you to let go and trust the Way of Breath.

Learning is an infinite journey through which the breath continues to guide us. Your breath will ride with you into the sunset of your life.

Breath has shown me the light and the dark of me, and taken me deep into my heart. I unfold like the eternal lotus flower, and just when I think I'm there and can go no further, I am humbled again, as if starting at the very beginning. I'm always the student and Life is always the teacher. I master aspects just for a moment, and crawl through others like a beggar. This is the way it is.

Perhaps we are all masters, pretending to have forgotten just for the fun of not-knowing, so that we can relearn the most magnificent thing there is to learn about — your 'Me'.

All I have to offer is what I've learned, and if it sounds good so far, perhaps you will stay a while longer. This is the bread I have to break with you, the wine I wish to share. Take a bite and a sip and be nourished from your roots to your soul. It's the work of the angels and works in the hands of a child. It's no more complex than the human psyche and as simple as drinking water. Walk with me to the next page and let me introduce you to yourself.

> But first, go to www.iloveyoume.co.uk/book-bonuses to download your complimentary "Breathe & Receive" audio meditation and your companion workbook.
>
> ~Thank you

"Hello Me"

Hello. Have you met Me?

"Hello, Me."

Go on, say it out loud, so that you can hear it. With your hand on your heart, affirm that these words are meant for you — *"Hello, Me!"*

It probably feels weird to you, to say that to yourself **internally**, never mind **Out Loud!**

In normal everyday life we tend to say it to everyone; dogs, cats, strangers, people we pass in the park, other people's babies, and our plants. We may even say it to the big, wide world when we wake up "Hello World!"

How many times could we catch ourselves inadvertently saying hello to inanimate objects like the car of our dreams in a showroom window, the ineffably high stack of washing up that you're about to tackle, a picture of a person in a magazine that you like the look of, or the designer dress to die for on the sale rack — hel-loooo! But how weird is it that when we turn our attention 180 degrees from out there to back here, towards our own self, and say "hello" that it feels uncomfortable and awkward?

Most people have never ever done it, and when I invite them to say it, usually for the first time, they hesitate, feel embarrassed, shy or even completely drop-dead ashamed. Some people say it and the words are left hanging in the air like a bad smell that no one wants to claim. Some people refuse, point-blank and seal their lips so tightly thin; jaw clenched and barely breathing, or choke on the unwanted lump of emotion that it brings to their throat. We seem to have some notion that talking to ourselves means that we're mad, stupid, selfish, or worse, that we're childish. The very idea of it can make us feel paranoid and scared.

Acknowledgment

What's so bad, wrong or weird about acknowledging ourselves with a simple 'Hello'?

'Hello' is a simple and universal form of acknowledgement. A very important verbal confirmation that **one has been recognised** as being present and **here,** necessarily preceding any further communication and engagement.

We live in a world where we tend to look to others for validation, for a measure of our own worth or value, or to be approved of and feel that we're loved. It's normal. We are constantly seeking, mostly pretending one way or another, that we are not **needy** and don't **need** anyone's attention when in truth we do, and we are. The fact is: We need attention, and will become unwell and unhappy with the lack of it.

Think of yourself when you were a child. How would it have been if no one ever gave you any kind of attention? What if nobody looked at you, or touched you, or listened to you? What if no one ever spoke a single word to you? Do you think you would feel happy and loved? Do you think you would be thriving and healthy right now? Alive even? Really... imagine a world where you receive no attention *whatsoever*...

The answer to all of these questions is of course 'NO'. You probably wouldn't have a sense that you even existed; you'd be like a ghost.

It's an absolute necessity that we receive confirmation and validation of our existence if we are to continue living.

"A hundred years ago, about 99% of babies in orphanages in the United States died before they were seven months old...babies died, not from infectious diseases or malnutrition; they simply wasted away in a condition called "Marasmus." Sterile surroundings didn't cure it; having enough food made no difference. These babies died from a completely different kind of deprivation: lack of touch"
—Health Touch News by Ben E. Benjamin, PhD

Every living creature needs attention to survive. Pets and young children have no shame or embarrassment in seeking out attention and affection when they need it, and this need does not disappear just because we've gotten older. Yet, why is it that as adults we most often feel ashamed of needing attention, either trying to avoid the need completely or else asking for our needs to be met in round-about, backwards, encrypted or manipulated ways?

Need To Be Significant

Some people wait all their lives to be given something of significance, great value or meaning; a token that they are themselves significant and valuable to somebody in their life. Some people have been given tons of material objects as a show of affection and love, yet they still feel unloved and not significant at all. We look to gain work, status, some kind of recognition. We try to win significance or earn it. We want significance from an ideal mate, our soul mate; the Significant Other. We interact, build relationships and grow families. We want to be loved for all that we are and are not, and so go about bending ourselves into all kinds of shapes, squeezing ourselves into all kinds of costumes and masks, trying on other people's identities for size to see if we like the fit better, so as to be significant.

"Would a bee try to act like a flower?"
— Prem Rawat 1995, Alexander Palace, London

It's a no-brainer, but our primary relationship starts at home. It's the last place we look, even though we see our face daily.

Acknowledgement Begins A Relationship

Wouldn't it be easier if we were honest with ourselves and got straight to the point? Do you need to be acknowledged by some kind of connection from others? Either talked to or listened to, seen, touched or empathised with in your life? Do you need some attention to help get you out of your current rut? Would it give you a good reason to heal old wounds and current maladies and to help you thrive, so that you could feel more loved?

If the answer is yes, then try it again. Say, out loud, just for the sake of your own ears, and say it so that the 'You' that needs acknowledgment and significance is allowed to hear it.

"Hello Me."

Breathe deeply and let the words sink in. Drink them in like a sweet, delicious medicine. Start a relationship with you by simply saying, "Hello."

We Need To Come Home

You need, whether you like it or not, kicking and screaming in blue-faced denial if you must, to come back to you, come back to the source of How and When it all started. It's time to face what you've been very skilfully avoiding: Your Self.

You Are Your Birthday Present

You were given this 'me' on the day of your birth. You came here **for free!** Somebody somewhere must have made a wish, whether it was your soul, God, your mother and father, your siblings or beloved, a call was made, an order was placed, and like magic you were delivered!

Do you ever have the kind of feeling as if there's a little 'You' looking out of your eyes at the world, trying to be in command of this big, earth-body suit, walking around on this strange planet wondering what you're doing here? Maybe it's just me, but I've had feeling this since I was a small girl and I still have it now. It's all quite surreal really, yet I call it My body, My life, My mind, My, my, my...

Where has your focus been? Where has your attention been mostly directed, that's brought you to where you are now in your life? Do you know? Do you know exactly where you are right now, and how you are?

It's my guess that you just think you do, but in reality you have a gnawing, unexplainable frustration, dissatisfaction, disappointment, disillusionment or dis-ease (disease). Maybe some things in your life are ok, or even doing well, but still there's an overall sense that something's just not right; that you're losing your grip and you urgently need an upgrade, or a way out? Maybe your health is suffering; your important relationships, or work, or your creativity and purpose are intangible and unfulfilled? Ultimately, like I said in the beginning, is there a sense that something's missing that you cannot figure out, and it's driving you crazy and making you feel deep down, irrecoverably lost and sad?

Welcome to the club of most of humanity! You are not alone, despite the glossy illusion that tricks your eyes and your mind into believing that it's *just you.*

Come back now, connect to your Self, the precious one that you lost contact with. Together we're going to find that very thing that makes your heart sing. But you have to be willing, just for a short while, to be given to, to be led, and to set down your baggage.

You left home a long time ago, and I don't mean your parents' house or the place you were raised. Do you remember when it happened? You've been trying really hard. You work hard to be here. You made it through childhood, you survived teenage-hood, and now you're out in the world trying to do your bit, to belong, to fit in and participate meaningfully in some way within this rapidly shifting world.

To get by in this world, to get what you wanted and needed in your childhood, clever, genius, little you devised strategies, but those creative strategies don't seem to apply anymore. It's not safe to be naive and it's dangerous to be innocent.

Whilst all this may seem overwhelming, all it takes it to start with a "Hello Me," Breathe and Receive and let the connection be made. It's a hook-line we throw in, allowing us to draw ourselves closer for the next step.

Tara Trilogy – Part 2

For the first half of my life I felt like a visitor from another star system observing instead of participating; watching the strange happenings and interactions around me while trying to blend in and not feel too weird! I was waiting for someone, or something, to either come get me, give me the feeling of inclusion and belonging, or else to take me the hell out of here! I would wait on top of high hills, roof tops or ladders calling for **them out there** to take me home, as if I'd been left here by mistake, or worse, dumped here as a punishment. (I'm sure some of you can relate) My University friends called me 'Starry Tara'. I was 'out there'.

I was given this opportunity to Exist as a **_gift._** My soul plays a part on this grand stage we call the world, dressed in a Tara outfit with means to express and experience, think and evaluate, grow and evolve with the rest of my species. I thought I was here to figure out the rules, to learn to adapt, to belong and contribute, but I didn't know How? Luckily, those who know, tapped me on the shoulder and said the answers aren't out there, they're in here, and pointed me back, inwards, towards myself. And then I realised I'd been carrying the gift around from one place to another, wanting to feel acknowledged, loved and understood by others, but I hadn't yet opened the parcel of Me, for myself.

I spent a long time judging the packaging, looking at the box without unwrapping. Was I beautiful enough? Did I get a good deal or was I shortchanged in the looks department? Were others given better features than me, cuter smiles, cuter curves? Was I too bottom-heavy, or too light and fluffy-headed? I should be taller, no smaller, thinner but not too thin. Are other people accepting me? Am I accepting myself? Can I succeed or have I already failed because I didn't look like much to me? Unconsciously I trapped 'me' inside whilst I sought to please people and did what I could to play the game, blend in and get by. It's as if I thought I was a basket.

Being A Basket Case

I already had a family that filled some space in my basket, but there was still more space that needed filling. So I took this fairly empty basket of 'My Life' out into the world, shopping. I placed friends and boyfriends in my basket, a job and money and pretty clothes. I placed spiritual teachings and books and schools, and positive affirmations to make my life cool. And, even though I smiled and laughed a lot, I still wasn't completely happy. Why does my basket feel so empty?

When I finally turned and met me, I realised my basket, my life, came ready packed with all the best things I would need for this sojourn on earth. It also came loaded with extra special treasures; treasures that I find only when I make it my mission to find them. I am a gift that came complete; a present for myself to unwrap and explore. I haven't finished yet, my gift hasn't expired.

What's more is that when I wish for something, which I believe I don't yet have... I find that the **very thing** I wished for was already placed inside this basket, pre-packed, waiting for me to find it! My wish was pre-given. It was Pre-sent! My wishes are part of my Present ME!

Like a treasure trail that lasts a lifetime, if I acknowledge my senses and follow them inward, I'm led straight to the gold and gems of my life. This present of Me is magic that way!

For example, as a child I wished to be psychic, to see auras and energy. Guess what...? That was already who I am and was yet to become.

I always wanted to be beautiful. I thought I wasn't. I wished for it. I cried for it. Until one day I began to look more closely, and then I noticed it. I am already beautiful in a 'Tara' kind of way. How could I not see that?

I wished most of all to meet the love of my life and experience TRUE unconditional Love in this lifetime. And, guess what... Life already had it planned out for me. I just had to keep unwrapping, keep living, keep feeling, learning and breathing my way along the trail in total trust. I had to become ready to receive. Life showed me True Love. It's the most brilliant. I feel very lucky! It was always inside me.

It's your birthday present because you need to stay present

So have you opened Your Birthday present? Have you seen what's pre-packed inside of you to fulfil all your needs and make your dreams come true? If you don't believe me, suspend your doubts a while. "I've looked!" you might say, "and I got a bum deal!"

Like a child hiding in the cupboard waiting to be found, the excitement wore off. Alone he/she sits in the dark feeling unloved because You stopped looking for him/her! Grief has filled your inner rooms and the doors have rusted shut.

Right here and now, every moment, receive the gift that keeps on giving. Every time that you show up, open handed, ready to receive, it shall be given. Knock and the door shall be opened. And, because you really are still a child, a child of Mother Nature and a child of the bigger force of Creation, no high-folluted, big booted, know-it-all grown up will fit through the door. It's made only for the sincere to fit through, the humble of heart; like a child who wanders into the garden of paradise because curiosity and wonder led him there. For a heart that is hungry and a mind that thirsts for more, be willing to leave your cleverness at the door.

"You had me at 'Hello."
—The Colour of Money (film)

Do You Want A Meaningful Relationship?

Of course you do, so let's start the bonding process with a surrendered "Hello... Hello Me"

And breathe Innnnnnnnn......and receive.........and ahhhhhhhhh.

Hello me.

There you are, first step taken.

It's gets better and better...

Baby Steps

Step 1 is so simple, and it's for this reason that the very first step is often missed. That can be the downfall of all other great plans and good ideas. Connection to yourself and your life essence is the foundation for your life. If you don't have this step in place, what's your life built upon?

I'll tell you. It's built on all those conditions and belief system imprints you inherited in your conception, birth and childhood — arrrrghhh!

It's built upon illusion, and thinking and ideas.

It's built upon something, up there, out there, like castles in the air. What goes up must come down, eventually.

Our thoughts, however wonderful, magnificent and cleverly crafted do not and will not serve us unless they have a platform of reality from which to sprout into solid, material form. Ideals without this basis are imaginations. They are dreams and wishes, hopes and heart break for the uninitiated and naive. Beautiful you - We are still children; evolving. We know not what we do most of the time. We make it up as we go along. We follow the lead of others who also know not what they do, just because they have a handsome CV (curriculum Vitae), a fantastic Mission Statement, a lot of money, or fame and celebrity.

I'm not suggesting you stop following and listening to others.

HOWEVER - the importance and absolute necessity of Step 1 is...

Connect With What Is

The immediate.

The present.

Your present.

You.

Plug in and stay there!

Do This Now

Would you be willing to love yourself enough to promise not to abandon your 'Me' at this point?

It takes practice and a commitment to re-train yourself to stay connected to you. The habit has been to search outwards for love, answers and knowledge all this time. Please don't give up yet just because your perspective has now shifted 180 degrees and your head feels sort of funny?! Say out loud with your hands on your heart

"I Now promise that I will not abandon you again, Me. I promise to connect with you every day, Me, because you need and deserve to be connected to."

Now breathe in all those words, thoughts and feelings...and ahhhhh...

Let go effortlessly.

Thank you.

Please now go to your workbook and do Step 1 Exercise 1 so that you can practise your connection with yourself.

~Thank you!

Loving Reminders

- STEP 1 -
I LOVE MYSELF ENOUGH TO CONNECT WITH ME

- ❖ B~R~E~A~T~H~E and R E C E I V E and **feel**

- ❖ I Connect within to the omnipresence of **Life** that is already happening for me, to me and with me.

- ❖ The person I most need to establish a loving relationship with is me.

- ❖ Life is constantly establishing a loving relationship with me by throwing me *a Life-line of Breath every* moment of every day. I need to take it.

- ❖ I need attention to survive and to thrive. I need connection. It's natural and right to need it.

- ❖ Connecting with and acknowledging myself every day feels wonderful.

- ❖ I begin with 'Breathe and Receive,' bring my hands to my body and say, "Hello Me."

- ❖ I am my Birthday present!

- ❖ My picnic basket for life came pre-packed. Everything I need is inside me.

- ❖ My wishes are pre-sent, like a present wrapped inside gift that I Am.

- ❖ Wishes come true by staying in the present moment.

- ❖ My first nature is to receive, like my first breath when I was born.

- ❖ If I want to receive more from life, I must first learn to receive my life.

- ❖ When I learn to unconditionally receive life, everything I want will follow.

- ❖ Life never abandons me, it's me who abandons life.

- ❖ I receive life as unconditionally as it is given to me.

And when you're down with that, we can then continue with the other 6 steps... YAY!

True Stories

"'I love you, me' practices were a revelation to me, a life re-awakening process. It softened my prejudiced, pre-determined, stubborn me. It tackled my preconceived ideas and my way of life, and it diluted my ego (which has been my main enemy). It has helped me reconnect with my true self, accept love, and cherish my Self in its weaknesses and struggles...

Only when you accept your struggling self, make peace with it, love and heal it then you will be able to love others and others will be healed...Like in Ho'ponopono when one accepts full responsibility of what is happening and to embrace, heal and nurture the inner child within oneself who has been broken, hurt, and burdened with all the accumulated pains sorrows guilt and sufferings, asking to let go, then things start to change.

During each "I love you, me" session, I try to identify the issues that are troubling me, to let go of attachments, mourn, try to release them ... I still feel better after each session

I learned that when you perpetuate your problems they become acute suffering. When you accept them and embrace them...they will ooze out slowly but surely.

I love you me is a wonderful healing modality. It is a return to oneself, to acceptance, to full responsibility, to peace within, to a cherished silence, to connection with the source, to an amazing state of grace, to full awareness and all presence. With it I am transcending the third dimensional issues and sufferings.

Ultimately when one feels complete, connected within, in a constant state of love, compassion and bliss... One will be listened to, miracles will start to happen — this is my humble experience. It is a continuous cleansing process that I will continue to do and I am getting better at it with time..."

—Hani Raydan, Abu Dhabi, UAE

"THANK you I love you for this amazing meditation, "Breathe and Receive" - It came at the perfect time. I was about to breast feed Isidora, so she and I listened to it together — it was the most magical feed I have experienced so far. Both of us were so present, no kicking from her, no doubts or neediness from me! Just both of us loving ourselves, our bodies and being here in this plane together. Exquisite. Thank you thank you thank you."

—Jenny, South Arica

Step 2
Transformational
Decisions

LOVING MYSELF ENOUGH
TO CHOOSE ANEW

"The Power Of Choice"

"It is in your moments of decision that
your destiny is shaped."
— Tony Robbins

Is Choice A Power?

Before we do anything, we first choose to do it — like reading this book for example. You have already decided that this book is worth reading, or at least taking a look at, for the insight you hope to gain. Even if someone gave it to you as a present because they thought you could use a self-help manual (LOL!) It's your choice whether you honour their wish and read the book.

No-one else is making   your   eyes   move   along   this   page Hahaha!

It's the same with everything else in our lives, whether it's about our happiness, health, wealth, work, love, relationships and spiritual path; anything concerned with our current daily reality is a direct result of our choices. No matter whose advice or whose orders you may have followed, you chose to follow it. Let me say it again - *Everything that you have in your life NOW is a direct result of your decisions and choices.* Some of them you made knowingly, others you don't remember making because it was a long time ago, and some of them are totally oblivious to you.

Making Decisions From What We 'Know' And Don't Know

We each have a unique combination of filters in our perspective, according to what we believe we deserve, want or need. We make decisions based upon our 'greater want', or what we believe we are allowed to have, be, or do in our lives.

For instance; we decide we **can't** do or have something because we think it's too expensive, or because we are not good enough, or because somebody more powerful than us would disapprove and possibly hurt us.

We think we **can** do, be, or have something when we have certain proofs and permissions in our beliefs that fuel us. For example, if your father was successful at earning money or running a company, that would be a valid proof that it's possible for you to attain the same; you've been given permission to succeed. If you won a sports day race in school when you were seven years old, you have a proof in your memory that you are a 'winner'. Our various filters inform us what we can or can't, what's possible or impossible, what's allowed and what's not allowed for us to achieve or be. It doesn't matter if it's a 'can' or a 'can't'; a positive or negative belief, it's still a limited knowledge base from which we gather our intelligence from, and upon which we form our decisions.

Perspectives and filters are often hard to change because the beliefs are so deeply ingrained. Over time they become rigid. The belief system is a difficult place to successfully navigate, especially since some of our biggest, most controlling bottom-line beliefs are totally invisible to us. We've lived with limitations or gaps in our understanding for such a long time, or even our whole lives, so that we don't know what we don't know. We have blind spots that we don't even know we're blind to.

"There are things we know that we know. There are known unknowns. That is to say there are things that we now know we don't know.
But there are also unknown unknowns.
There are things we do not know we don't know"
—Donald Rumsfeld, US Secretary of Defence

This is where we enter a dark chasm of 'not knowing' in our psyche. Here we get lost and lose perspective because we don't know how to claim back the power that other people seem to have over our lives. We don't even know how we lost it. How do you get out of the pit you're in when you don't know how you got there? When you're stuck in a rut, and you're not even sure what that rut is, how are you going to get out?

There's a gap in our knowledge that's scary to behold and seemingly impossible to enter. So instead of going into the unknown to make new discoveries and find our power, we tend to cling to the edge of the chasm and not venture further. Most of us don't even know that we're doing that, bless our souls. We just feel stuck.

For example, you might not know what it feels like to be unconditionally loved, and so you might be clinging to a relationship and living with very painful conditions because you can't face or cross the chasm of the unknown. Maybe you don't even know you have a choice here. Maybe you think this is all there is? Pain might be your normal in relationships.

You might believe you can be a millionaire and want to be one, but because you have no actual clue how that feels or what that looks like, the darkness of not knowing will keep you in poverty, or creating less than you deserve. Maybe you feel doomed, or destined, or just stuck?

You might not even know that these blocks in your heart or psyche exist, but for some reason you still can't seem to get from the 'Known' painful reality to the not-yet-known 'New Reality'. So if you don't know what you don't know, how can you make an impactful, transformational decision? It seems impossible does it not?

And why is it that with some things we feel we have a choice, and others we don't?

How We Lose Our Power – The Blame Game

The 'Good guys' versus the 'Bad guys' is the most classic story line. It's the blueprint of a made up reality that's embedded in our psyche, and from which virtually ALL other stories originate.

The narrative contains 3 important characters.

1. The innocent victim(s)

2. The Hero(s) that must overcome the

3. The Villain, Bad Guy, Darkness or the Unknown.

In this narrative, but not necessarily in this order, we have the 'evil' or 'bad' people who do XYZ bad things. We generally want them stopped, killed, and/or made to pay for what they've done. The usually poor, innocent, or helpless victims have no choice but to suffer the tyrant's wrath and reign and tend to need to be rescued from them. We are taught to hate the villain, to blame him or her and wish for their demise so that we can enjoy seeing the victim live happily ever after. We prefer to sympathise with the victims because we relate to their pain and suffering and want it to end; typically. That's not true for everyone, but whatever side we're routing for the fact remains that we make a separation between what's good and what's bad, and we choose a side.

Then the hero arises! The one who decides to take responsibility for the whole situation and bring it into balance, alone, carrying the weight and the fate of the world on his or her own shoulders. We cheer him or her on until the villain is slain, the day is won, the people are saved and the innocent can go back to being helpless and dependent on the hero to someday rescue them again.

NOW, LET'S TAKE THIS NARRATIVE STRUCTURE PERSONALLY.

Even if this is not your preferred version of events, let us suspend all belief for a moment and wonder if, in fact, all alternative versions of our own narratives are born of this primitive pattern?

Let's ask ourselves - What has this story got to do with me?

Who's the Victim in my story? Who's the Bad Guy and the Hero?

And if it is true, how could the victim be a victim no longer? How could the villain be transformed from 'Bad Guy' to 'Good Guy' so that the fighting can end? Or, at least his powers be neutralised and made ineffective? How can I win? How could I give the Hero a break from always having to save the day, take the brunt, and sacrifice himself in the name of Do-Gooding? Would the hero like to quit carrying the whole burden alone?

What if everyone could get on board with the objective of getting the heck out of this melodrama, to go have fun instead and create happier, more peaceful stories with a more useful contribution to our lives? What kind of a story would that be?!! A boring one! All the drama gone? No bad guy? You would want your money back if this was Hollywood.

We All Love A Bit Of Drama

So, isn't it true that we all love a bit of drama? The more believable it is, and the more impossible the hero's mission seems, the more we become engrossed, get the ride, experience the thrill and feel that it was a good investment of our time. We all love to have that righteous justified feeling of victory whilst casting shame and blame upon those we deem deserving of it. It satisfies some egocentric part of our self. We give ourselves credit for doing so, thinking that we're good people in contrast to those 'bad' or 'wrong' others.

But, how would it be if we ended the drama in our own lives by taking back the power from the situation and from others, and redirecting it? Can we re-direct the movie of our own lives, give each player in our cast a different role, and create a whole new narrative where everybody wins? Of course we can, if we want to...

The 5 Elements of Transformational Decisions

I believe there are 5 vital Elements to making a Transformational Decision. Here is the first one…

ELEMENT ONE
'OWN YOUR POWER'

When we were young, grown-ups had control of our lives. They 'owned' us. We were innocent as to what was wanted and expected of us, and helpless to our situation and circumstances. Sometimes, or often, we were victims to punishment, unfairness and unpleasantness that we probably felt forced to endure at the time. It's true. The reality of innocent victims is true, to this extent.

However, as we grow we form our own ideas, gather our own identity and strengths and start to embody a sense of power. Can you remember the times in your childhood when you decided that you were going to gain control of your own life? Mostly it happened in stages. For some of us we were very little indeed, far too little to make adult, well informed, and insightful decisions for ourselves. But we tried nonetheless, out of sheer desperation sometimes to escape the situations that we were helpless or victim to. We sought independence, help or relief, and many of us are still unconsciously repeating the escape patterns that we fell back on as children with limited knowledge. Are we truly, fully independent yet? Did we escape? Are we free?

Some of us didn't want to claim independence. Perhaps childhood and helplessness was all too comfortable and growing up seemed like a lot of unnecessary hassle, or too difficult. In both cases, who successfully taught us how to be a proper, responsible, empowered, loving and happy grown up?

If you're not fulfilling your potential as a free and empowered adult making new choices, how come?

We Get Comfortable Stuck In Our Rut

We want change. We want better jobs, more money, a different body, look or hair style; a different car or better life style. All people want more love in their lives, more meaning, and generally more peace and joy. We all want change.

Except we don't! We look out of our window, either of our home or our soul; wishing, wanting, hoping, praying, dreaming and visualising something other than the situation or circumstance we currently have. We want a magical, fairytale kind of change...

Except we don't. We are quite comfortable stuck in our ruts. Change takes effort to DO something new, to think outside of our cozy paradigm. For example; I'm a single Mum, I'm a brick layer, I'm poor, I'm ill, I'm overweight, I have this inadequate thing that I'm comfortable with because deep, deep down I believe I am destined to be single/sick/poor/a grafter/overweight/unloved/unhappy. The list goes on; you get the idea.

It's not a *nice* rut to be in but somehow we feel it suits us, we fit into it nicely! It's what we know. It's much easier to dream and to wish that it were different, than to make significant change happen.

There are tons of ways we try to create change. Surely being positive is good? Yes, of course, except when it becomes a sticking plaster or a manhole cover to hide or cleverly avoid the deeper issues. By all means, look on the bright side and make great changes in your day to day. Just ensure that it is not at the expense of the poor little, innocent you trapped at the bottom of your rut.

Our blue-print and conditioned psychology (that was created by the people in our past) seeks to separate issues so as to resolve them. Leave home, or leave your partner. Push your parents away so as not to become like them. Push away the helpless part of yourself in order to succeed. Ignore the pain and it'll go away. Deny the villainous dark side, close your eyes and it'll disappear. If we take a quick glance at what our parents did to solve problems and pain, and what their parents did, and beyond, we might want to ask ourselves if we're still applying the same method of solving, and if it **really works?** This is where our innocent inner child learned it from. We are effectively using the same methods to attain a different result generation after generation. No wonder things are still a mess.

Could we perhaps stop separating the hero, victim and villain roles, learn to integrate and live with our entire psychology? Because heroes who exert massive amounts of will power, determination and effort to succeed at climbing of out the comfortable (but uncomfortable) rut are fallible to forgetting something crucial. The hero might plough on ahead, climbing not just out of the pit, but continuing up, up the mountain to the summit of success. Once there they feel the elation but also the anti-climax. Did they forget something, or someone? Did they forget the most important part of themselves, the innocent, victim, the child who's left buried at the bottom?

Gulp — Maybe.

Did your hero, who strives hard to survive, realise that the very darkness he/she is trying to escape from is his/her shadow, which is attached for life to your heels? Did your hero notice that his/her shadow sometimes falls over other people, casting an apparent darkness over them, creating **the illusion that they are the bad guy,** the very antithesis and rejected part of your good self?

You can reach success **on behalf of** your poor-little-me while he/she remains abandoned, or you can bring him/her with you. You can recognise your shadow and take it with you, heroically owning it so that no-one else, big or small, becomes overcast as you block out their light. The two can join forces, not compete.

Do you want to stay in the chasm of your rut? You may hold on to self-righteousness if you want, or your claim to life's unfairness. Do you want to keep a comfortable sense of helplessness, victimhood and grief? Or, would you prefer to move into place of intense harmony and peace instead?

Breathe and Feel for the answer.

Would you be willing to love yourself enough to illuminate the 'not-knowing' void of darkness, cross the gap in the mind that does not know how, and close the chasm of helplessness? Could you love yourself enough to build a bridge of new possibility?

And after all these questions, I have just one more....

If it's indeed true that we do possess the power of choice to transform the drama, (or karma), that we find ourselves in, would you be willing to Love yourself enough to do so?

Then this is where to start.

Who is the owner of your life? Who is the owner of you? Go to Step 2 Exercise 1 in your workbook to discover who's got your power and how to get it back.

~ Thank you!

"When we consistently suppress and distrust our intuitive knowingness, looking instead for authority, validation, and approval from others, we give our personal power away."
— Shakti Gawain, Author

ELEMENT TWO
'RESPONSIBILITY'

Let's explore the next key element that enables transformational decisions and radical shifts in our reality. So, let's see. If you could ACTUALLY change the biggest problem in your life, would you do it? Are you getting some kind of benefit from your problem or pain? Or better, are you still waiting to get the bigger gain that you want more, keeping your problem as a bartering aid until you get it?

Are we just willing to make a good show of wanting change, when in truth, subconsciously, we are more invested in keeping attachments to our pain, suffering, fears and concerns because actually it reaps quite profitable rewards? Time spent in pain is an investment we make, because we subconsciously believe that it will pay off later and we will be significantly rewarded somehow. (Clue: Significance is a big key here) Do you want to find out?

PAIN = DIVIDENDS

Just out of curiosity, test which of the following might apply to your Pain investment.

Do This Now

Please read this aloud…

"*I am still suffering from* _____ fill in the blank) because:

(Tick the ones that arouse some kind of emotional response in you. Be honest! And, if you can, adopt a playful attitude. Let's make light work of this exercise. It's quite funny to realise what sneaky games we play with ourselves)

1. It makes me look like I'm a good person because I've suffered for something.

2. Feeling pain earns me points with my spouse /children /pets /friends church/community /God.

3. I fit in with everyone else. I'm more normal and easily acceptable.

4. It gives me something to talk about.

5. It makes me look strong to be able to deal with it so well and for so long, and suffer in relative silence. I don't want people feeling sorry for me. I'm proud of my strength and tolerance to pain and suffering.

6. I'm too weak and helpless to change. I need other people who are more grown up than me (mum /dad /partner /child /God /the doctor/the state etc.) to hold me and look after me.

7. I don't want to take responsibility for this pain. I want to stay young, innocent, naive   and childlike.

8. It gets me out of being powerful. Being powerful is hard. It's easier not to change.

9. It's the world's fault, God's fault, Mum's fault, Dad's fault, abuser's fault, government's fault, devil's fault. It's somebody's fault that I'm like this. I am a victim.

10. It's gets me attention. People/a particular person, fuss over me.

11. I can say that I don't like the attention, but they give me energy that I need.

12. It gives me significance. I'm more important because when something is the matter with me, I matter more to others.

13. If I save it and store it all up well, I can pass it down as a legacy of my love and protection to my children and grandchildren that I suffered for them so they could be happy.

14. My suffering is to make other people realise their fault, and until they see that they are to blame and owe me some responsibility, I can't get well /can't be happy /can't change.

15. Life is suffering. I'll get my redemption and rewards in heaven.

16. I'm waiting for them to say sorry to me. I need someone to recognise my pain and suffering first.

17. I don't know. I just am and I have no clue. I haven't really thought about it. I suffer needlessly.

18. It's easier just to get on and ignore my pain and suffering than to face the real deeper issues and wrongs of my past.

19. If I just keep doing what I'm doing, and try harder, it will eventually turn out all right, I'm sure of it. It's worth it now because my pain and suffering will get me what I want in the long run.

20. I am my suffering. I don't know who I am without it.

21. My God doesn't want me to be free from suffering. I am loved like this.

22. I've got used to feeling sorry for myself. It's become my normal and it entitles me to have a tantrum every now and again and yell at others for not doing more for me. I am justified.

23. I enjoy competitive suffering, I have to suffer more than my partner/mother/father/child etc., to gain significance. Whenever they tell me their problems mine are always bigger.

Having considered all these possible payoffs of your pain and suffering, (feel free to add your own) it begs the questions... How is that working out for you? Is your investment worth it? Are you winning?

The list shows all the different ways that we may have avoided taking responsibility for ourselves. It's what we've opted for instead, without realising, because we innocently or naively believed it would be the best way to behave to get the results we needed. In other words, it was the most effective solution as decided by our inner child. It's what we saw others around us doing and we learned to apply the same tactics. Except, as tactics go, is it realistically paying off?

I bet you were the kind of child who often felt responsible for others. And I bet that the majority of the people you felt responsible for either let you down or eventually betrayed you in some way emotionally. And now as an adult, when you need to be responsible for yourself in life, somehow you feel incapable and disempowered. It's as if the little child in you is still trying to be the grown-up one, but has never learned how to take considered, empowered and loving responsibility because there were none or few role models to show you how to do that. Perhaps we shouldered the pain and responsibility for those who didn't know how to? Perhaps it's on our shoulders because someone bigger than us put it there?

This is a super important chapter in your life, and in this book. It is not to be skipped over. **You have this opportunity to create a radical transformation in your hands right now for a reason.**

Freedom

Perhaps the reason could be that we, the rest of the universe and people of Earth that are with you right now in the great collective-consciousness scheme of things, want a different reality. We all want freedom. We could do with every little drop, every being, every soul, to own their fair share of the cleaning up so that we can ALL experience more love, true relief, happiness, good health and wellbeing. By owning our own pain and unconscious thoughts, feelings and actions, we might create more integration, connectedness and union between us. Is humanity done with all the suffering, pain and sickness yet? *Are we done with waiting for someone else to do it for us?* If we start now it'll be like waste re-cycling and organic food, it'll catch on. It won't take long to become the new norm for us all to be wonderfully, lavishly, selfishly happy by deciding to take responsibility for our own love and happiness and healing our own pain.

Or perhaps, that picture is too grandiose for you, and you've got enough to deal with on your own plate today, never mind thinking about the rest of the world.

Whether you want freedom for yourself, or for the world, I love you. Thank you for being here and reading these words. Thank you for taking the time to question the real motives behind your current situation. Thank you for being vulnerable, transparent and honest with yourself. You deserve total honesty, up-front clarity and no more hidden agendas. You are worth changing habits for. You are worth bringing in out of the cold, out of the war, out of your hell and suffering, out of the dark cupboards where the little you hides for safety. You are worth saving!

Thor or Ironman won't do it for you. Superman died. The messiahs came and went. Is it worth more waiting for a 'someday' hero, or are you ready to Get Yourself Unstuck?

It's your turn! If you think about it, when we believe we are helpless and incapable and give the cap of responsibility to someone else, we give up our rights to have power and authority over our own lives. We put that power into someone else's hand. Probably the person's hand whom you most resent. Is that what you want to do?

Taking full responsibility for your own LIFE is to truly treasure and maximise the *miracle* that you have in your hands. Responsibility gives you power. Then your 'Me' can feel secure, safe and cared for. You can start anew.

"With Great Responsibility Comes Great Power!"

And what if some amazing, unconditionally loving force that feels bigger and more powerful than you, is also there for you, reaching out to you in every moment? Would you reach back to receive it and hold onto it? What if it's possible to form a bond of love with something that won't let you down, that you absolutely *know* is real — the bigger, very powerful, more loving, YOU?

I'll show you HOW.

> **Go to your workbook and do Step 2 Exercise 2 to find out who you've made responsible for you.**
>
> **~Thank you!**

ELEMENT THREE
'INDEPENDENCE'

Mastery Of Me

Let's look at what it means to be 100% responsible for your Me and how we claim our mastery and power.

Mastery means moving from being in a dependant, child-like state, towards independently meeting our own needs and realising our true nature and divine purpose. Then we grow to become inter-dependent. Like trees in a forest connected by both roots and branches which together support the greater whole, a strong-standing empowered and dependable person will make an impactful contribution to humanity's evolution.

Dependency

Dependency is making a default to the weaker position and saying, "I can't do this for myself." When we are three years old it might be our shoelaces that we can't do, but as we grow to adulthood is might be things like:

I cannot support myself financially. I need other people's, the bank's, the government's, charity money; to survive.

I cannot support myself emotionally, I need others to hold me, listen to me, feel sorry for me, help fix me and make me feel better.

I cannot support myself mentally; I need others to tell me what to do, to make my decisions, to advise me, to be the clever one on my behalf.

I cannot support myself sexually. I get myself into dangerous or unwanted situations. I need to hide, shut down or disown my sexuality because I don't feel safe.

I cannot protect myself; I need protection from someone. I need to be controlled or dominated by someone. I keep myself vulnerable.

I cannot support my physical health. I need to blame other people or other causes for my ill health. I need to give my illness to someone else to fix. I cannot take ownership of my own body and functions of it.

Perhaps you can think of some other areas of life where you/we live in dependency?

Now please go to your workbook, Step 2 Exercise 3 to learn exactly where you are still dependent on others for your health, wealth, or happiness

~ Thank you!

By doing that small exercise you have drawn out all the things that you are currently dependent upon. With dependency come feelings of struggle, always treading water, never making it to the other side. It's exhausting and uses a lot of our energy. Dependency also looks like an octopus with arms everywhere, grabbing for attention, help and support; being slippery and manipulative to get our needs met or to get what we want. Generally we're being controlling, often passively, so that others do our bidding.

It's an exhausting way to play because we tend to need to do *a lot* of things to keep *a lot* of people happy, things that we'd probably prefer not to have to do. Or we base it all on One special other to be everything for us that we are being helpless about. Ultimately we compromise.

How do you like that? How does that make you feel?

Independence

Independence looks like taking full, unequivocal ownership of all that we can call Me and Mine: My body, my mind, my feelings, my intuition, my love, my relationships, my money, my poverty, my home, my needs, my wants, my desires, my purpose, my meaning of life, my truth, my beliefs etc...

Taking 100% responsibility for your life and being independent **is not the same** as saying things like:

> "I will take all the blame for something going wrong in my life and beat myself up for being so stupid and try hard not to repeat my mistake."

Nor is it the same as saying,

> "I can't trust or rely on anyone else. I don't NEED anyone. I must do everything ALONE!"

It **is** being able to feel the fullness, power and arising sensation within us that exudes an "I CAN and I WILL" greatness of energy, even if we don't yet know HOW we will take 100% independent responsibility for our self – **yet.**

Being independent means prioritising to meet our own needs first. Desires come after. At this juncture, let us qualify needs. Shelter, water, food and warmth are our basic needs for physical survival. The following list is what I believe we need for mental, emotional and spiritual survival, and for our overall well-being. It's a recognised human need to actualise our potential, thrive and evolve.

NEEDS FOR NOT JUST SURVIVING, BUT THRIVING

Need for Connection - We need connection to Self, to Life itself and to others. We need connection to Truth; To something Absolute in nature; to measure our own existence by; to give us Meaning and Purpose so that we are not alone. It can also be described as a need for Divinity, or a trustworthy intelligence. Connection gives us Strength. In experiencing connection we may then experience Union. (Step 1 in this book will take care of this, and also re-calibrate you for healthy, fulfilling meaningful connections with others)

Need for Certainty - Certainty is the absolute knowing that something is definitely going to happen, or is happening, and also the need for surety that something we don't want, won't ever, ever, ever happen again. Certainty creates <u>Safety</u> and therefore gives a much needed grounding for <u>Faith</u>.

Need for Acknowledgement - The acknowledgment of being seen, heard, spoken to, touched and empathised with; a confirmation that we exist. Acknowledgment creates <u>Intimacy</u> and <u>Trust</u>. We need to feel understood; that someone knows us, that we are validated.

Need for Liberty - The freedom to be who we are, or choose to be. To be released from anything which is not in harmony with us, to be enslaved to nothing and no-one, internally or externally; to have ultimate permission, to be allowed to be who we are or want to be.

Need for Unconditional Love - We need to know, beyond a shadow of a doubt that we are loved, genuinely, without condition or judgment. That no matter what we do, think or feel, we are sacred and special to someone, forever, for good. In unconditional love fault does not exist. Unconditional love creates <u>Compassion</u> and <u>Understanding</u>.

Need for Appreciation - To receive recognitions of gratitude assures us that our life has *meaning* to another. Being appreciated feeds our need to feel valuable and <u>Valued</u>. Gratitude is an extreme expression of Positivity, Power, and Affirmation that we Can, and it IS possible. Gratitude gives us feelings of <u>Fulfilment</u>. Appreciation cultivates our need to contribute or be in <u>Service</u>.

Need for Home - Home is essentially shelter, physical and metaphysical. A place of belonging, respite, rest, ease and comfort. Home gives us the feeling of <u>Joy</u>, or contentment for no other conditional reason. It is another essential need. Home is a place to just BE in <u>Peace</u>, non-separate and whole.

Need to be in service – We need to contribute in order to have a meaningful role or purpose in life, to serve the Divine or share our gifts with others. We need a sense of <u>Purpose</u> for our lives to be apparently bigger than we are; to leave a legacy.

Taking Care Of Our Needs Independently

How would it feel if all of these needs were more than adequately met? Who could you be? What could you achieve? What would become possible for you then, that was previously impossible to conceive? How could the quality of your life change, or better still transform?

You might be jumping up and down inside, all excited with a giant 'YES!' in your eyes! But then what happens is… sooner rather than later, a little thought comes creeping in – "But *how?*"

This dreaded word "How?" can reduce you back to slumped and helpless. It can make you give up before you've got started. You can say:– "But I've tried and I have decided, and it didn't work!"

If this is you, then perhaps you don't really want to shift out of your current uncomfortable, comfort zone that I was just talking about earlier? Perhaps you'd rather stay dependant? Maybe you're not ready for what can happen next?

That's really okay, no one's judging you. You're the only one here right now, look around. No one else can see what you're reading and what's going on in your mind.

It's Your Choice

Everything you want and need **is** possible for you, or else you wouldn't be drawn to having it. (Remember how all our wishes are pre-packed) What we want seeks us as much as we seek it. Life is a two-way flow. You are going to have to get the things you want for yourself. It's your choice to grow bigger and do what is necessary so that you attain your independence. Unfortunately, no one else can do it for you.

I say that you are free to choose… but in reality that's not entirely true, because it's only a matter of time before the wheel of fortune and the circle of life comes back round again to knock on your door with another predicament that poses the same questions. Are you willing to stay in your helpless situation or will you take the current level of your discomfort as a sign that something *needs* to change?

How much discomfort can you *stand?!*

I'm not forcing you or trying to scare you. I love you, actually. I know just how you feel. It probably hasn't dawned on you that you do indeed have the power, or whatever it takes, to change your situation, problems, struggles in life, with nothing but your own hands, heart, mind and spirit.

Are you asking, "But how can I be independent and responsible for the fact that I have no relationship?" or "that I have no money, or that my Mum died or that my brother is ill, or my wife left me, or that I was abused, or that the world is so messed up?" etc...

It's not your fault, NO, most definitely not. Responsibility doesn't mean fault.

But, what if I showed you How by taking 100% independent responsibility for your needs, your happiness, your peace, your health, your wealth, your love; by making a committed decision to serve You and You alone, right now as your highest priority, you can transform anything!

Go now to Step 2 Exercise 4 to declare your independence

~ Thank you!

Have You Met How?

Are you feeling a glowing, expanding sensation of power inside your heart and belly as your body responds to the truth? Are you ready to ask some of the best questions ever?

"Would I be willing to love myself even more right now?"

"How can I love myself even more right now?"

"How can I give myself what I need to transform my situation right now?"

"How can I create what I really want in my life and be totally supported by others who want the same for me?"

How, please tell me?

When we ask 'How' with an open mind and heart to bring the answers we need, How appears - like a magic genie ready to grant our wishes. Conversely if we repeatedly say things like "But ***I don't know how,"*** with frustration and a negative heart and mind, then we block the inspiration, fortune and co-creative forces that want to meet our request. The door is effectively shut on our poor dear friend 'How'. Keep the door open for new possibilities and your genie 'How' will reveal all.

Now, here's the trick, you've got to stick with it. You've got to maintain your decision and focus.

Why would you do that? What's the benefit of making the effort?

Interdependence

Interdependence is when each tree stands alone because all the needs were met and the conditions right for it to grow strong and tall. Yet as it grew the roots interconnected with other roots of other trees and together they formed a matrix of mutual support. Interdependence is not created from a place of lack and therefore a need to lean upon another, but rather from strength, stability and an ability to make a greater contribution than one could make alone. Interdependence is where our highest dreams are realised, where we may become something greater, unified with the whole rather than remaining separate and isolated.

It's where our branches reach out and touch one another, feeling the companionship of strength; delighting in the mutual growth and expansion from our core, root source, and enjoying the liberation we feel flying high together in our power and on track with our destiny. We come into service; we fulfil our potential as human beings. We give up the right to be dependent and helpless, and we give up the right to be lone-wolfs believing that we must achieve everything in life, off of our own backs. That's simply not true, but we must be able to stand on our own two feet, in our own right, in our own power first.

First fulfil yourself.
Fill your own cup with contentment, love, joy and service 'til it runs over.
To thine own self be true.

Many years of personal experience and the witnessing of the world around me informed me, that when we try to serve others or the world before we serve ourselves we become empty and drained, having little or nothing left to give. We become martyrs. Even if we seem successful at selflessly giving, we can be left feeling unsatisfied, lacking, and believing we have not done enough. Commonly we think that if we just give a little bit more we will have the rewards of feeling content and happy.

If your gift is music, make it for yourself and for your own radiant joy! Then you can share it. If your gift is healing, heal yourself first and share what works. If you manage or direct, then manage and direct things in your own life so well that you walk your talk. If you love to do charity work, then do so because you have been the charity case you so benevolently gave to in the beginning. Learn how to give well by giving first to you.

As Gandhi so rightly said:

"Be the change you wish to see in the world."
—Ghandi

But don't be a Gandhi. This is no longer a time for self-sacrifice or martyrdom. Be the leader. Do as you would you would wish others to do. Be the light. Be the joy. Be the love you wish to see in the world. Be great, for your own fulfilment, and your greatness will spread.

ELEMENT FOUR
'PRIORITIES'

What's Your Priority?

At this moment in your life you are prioritising reading this book.

It has jumped the queue of other very important things to top position because you are in need of change. Your life needs a revolutionary change, not just a quick fix, and this is what's keeping you glued to these words. Something in you urges you forwards, what I call your inner divine wisdom, so that your logical brain will receive the messages it needs to hear and get all the elements it needs to make a new decision.

This next element is priorities.

The jobs at the top of the priorities list, those deemed most important, are the ones that get done. The want for some kind of change in your life is probably a priority right now, but does this want include the priority to love yourself more? If what's behind those things at the top of your list, urging that change, is a heap of negative self beliefs and judgements; too fat, too thin, too slow, too much, not enough, etc., then you will end up punishing yourself and reinforcing the pain that you feel. As a result, you will probably find the change to be either unachievable or much harder and more painful that it needs to be.

What if I told you that your soul steers your conscious mind? What if, despite having a heap of priorities on your 'to-do' list for happiness, you also have a heap of subconscious "To-do's" that are sabotaging your flow? A simple illustration of this could be; You want to go out on more dates with your husband but he's too busy with work/family etc, and you're too tired from your work/kids/caring for others etc, The priority to have a happy relationship and nurture your marriage takes second place to the needs and demands of other people. There's a silent saboteur at work.

Let's look at this on a more personal and deeper level.

"We want to change because we don't like ourselves. Often, we want to become someone we feel is more worthy of being honoured
— by ourselves and by others.
But to accomplish lasting transformation, the strongest tool we have is self-love"
—Brant Second, shamanic healer, and Mark Allen, six-time Ironman Champion

Subconscious And Systemic Priorities

Remember when you were younger and looking at the big wide world for the first time? Do you remember deciding what was most important to you? Was it being a Mum or Dad, was it being good and pleasing Mum or Dad, or was it something else, like running away, looking after someone, being a soldier, nurse, or pilot? What could you see for yourself that was certain?

We follow glimpses of what we know, on the road to the unknown. Where we see to step, we step. Where we see dark areas and shadows, we tend to avoid. As a small child we grasped certain aspects of life that were shown clearly to us by grown-up others. We could follow in those footsteps only as far as we could see our future taking us. However, we also saw things through small-person eyes, with purity and the wisdom of innocence still intact, so our perspective differed from the big people's more hardened and opinionated views around us. We had some innocent inner-sense of our own path amidst the path already laid before us.

I believe we were guided by our divine-self, showing us an alternative route. Our dreams and ideals hovered in front of us like a will-o'-the-wisp, leading us forwards, seeming real, becoming the stepping stones along our path. However, our intuitive guidance is meshed and entangled with the pre trodden paths of those who have gone before. This combination has formed the handholds for our climb to adulthood.

Now, let me side step a moment and tell you something more about this intuitive guidance that's at work in your life...the soul that is steering.

Remember what I told you about the conditioning of your parents and ancestry? And how their unresolved business plays out in your life since you are the next one in line to inherit the case? Well, believe it or not, we are, to a large degree playing out their unfinished stories and incomplete wants, desires and dreams too. It's as some unfulfilled part of them remains alive and lives through us, seeking to be put to rest along with their bodies. And so it is our befallen duty to act it out, even if it's not our true calling, and bring it to harmony and peace within us. Similarly, we tend to learn the tricks of our parents' trades, whether it's our passion or not, and often end up defaulting to their career paths, or similar life paths, until we work their stuff out of our system and find our own.

In the same vein, it's also true that we have particular gifts and talents passed down through the genetic lineages. Like the long warp threads on a loom these abilities remain constant in the family, but usually hidden under the crossing waft thread of the generation before us as the shuttle of time moves under and over in our family tapestry. Threads seem to skip a row as talents can skip a generation.

Both parts, the potential talents and the unfulfilled or unrealised dreams are in the blood none-the-less, and intelligently they seek to bring themselves out and have their day in court or their moment in the limelight during your lifetime.

Somehow we signed up for this deal, whether we remember it or not. Somehow, in the grand scheme of life it was deemed perfect that we slot into place amid these warp and weft threads of the others who came before us, as if it were somehow befitting to our own soul's evolutionary journey to pick up where they left off. How perfect would that be if it were true? Wouldn't that somehow make very deep sense, even if our brain can't quite yet figure it?

Your list of active, though mostly sub-conscious priorities would look like a mixture of both your ancestral patterns and your soul's inspirations. Wouldn't you like to find out what they are? How interesting would it be to see what's unconsciously playing out as an old priority and what your soul is urging and inspiring you to do next as a new one?

Go to the Step 2, Exercise 5 in your workbook. Complete the first 2 lists and come back.

~Thank you.

Comparing The Lists

Are there any old priorities from either list that are in conflict with your 'now' priorities? How many of them are you still living out from your young adult list? Are you still working from the same priorities list or have you successfully updated it with the same clarity that you had as a young person or child? And how might they be sabotaging what you want in your life now, despite the day to day effort you make to create what you want?

If you haven't satisfactorily achieved your top priorities in life by now, it will be difficult to achieve any of your other wants and needs, even with your best effort. There are forces at work in your subconscious that need to be worked out and resolved before you can move on. Conversely, but just as likely, are your top priorities consuming the majority of your time, energy and attention thus preventing you from achieving the others?

For example, being a wonderful parent may be one of your very top priorities, but when your children are grown and need less full time attention do you default to doing non-essential Mum or Dad activities rather than freeing yourself to do your 'now' priorities? Have you slipped into routines that once were supportive but are no longer necessary? It's a hard habit to break, and requires a realignment of purpose.

Or it might be that in the past you prioritised being poor because that had advantages or it made you fit in, but you're trying to become rich now whilst the old priority is still holding top spot? Or vice versa, you came from wealth but saw only trouble and betrayal, and so vowed to not be wealthy and prioritised avoiding becoming like your family? Or you want to be in a relationship, but you're subconsciously prioritising being single to protect yourself from being hurt like your mother or father, and therefore you're still alone? Or you prioritised helping others before yourself to avoid being selfish because people around you taught you that it's not a loveable trait?

What would you prioritise now if you loved yourself enough?

You know more now that you knew then. You are wiser, clearer, more practiced at life. You've had more experiences of what you don't want, to know what you do want. You've had more time to listen and look into your inner picnic basket and discover what life has waiting for you. What have you been wishing for? What is bubbling out of your basket to be manifested and realised in your life? What does the magic genie 'How' want to grant for you next? Ask and it shall be yours.

This next exercise is probably something that you want to spend time pondering over until you gain real inspiration about getting your priorities in order.

When you're ready, go back to the exercise and complete list 3 - your 'Now priorities'

~ Thank you!

THE FIFTH ELEMENT
'DEDICATION'

The fifth element of the transformational decision making process, the crucial part that holds it all in place, is to make a dedication. Your dedication is your ongoing commitment to maintain and act upon your personal revelations that you've experienced so far during this Step 2 process.

A dedication is also an energy that we send forward, like a trajectory path of what we want to achieve and how we want to feel on the other side. For instance, once the caterpillar has woven herself inside the cocoon, she is then dedicated to her transformation to become a beautiful butterfly, which means staying the journey of the apparent 'death' experience, having a re-birth then emerging from the cocoon to be her new self. A birthing mother must remain dedicated to the labour process so that she **actively** births her baby safely into the world. Dedication means focus, commitment and action.

In much the same way, we now need to make a dedication to your birthing process that will assist you in leaving behind your old definitions and deformations that have been a dragging pain and burden in your life so far, and create a carrier wave that surges you forward and out to the light at the end of the tunnel!

A dedication needs to be done with a whole-body consciousness, i.e., you are fully emotionally, mentally and spiritually dedicated to your physical life being experienced differently. It feels like a labouring rush or surge of energy that washes through you with a warmth or a might about it. It's the kind of feeling that needs to be honoured with your two feet planted firmly on the ground, engaged with the solidness of the earth and ready to step into the next action with heartfelt force to carry you forward into the not-yet-known part of your journey. It's how a baby might feel as she prepares to leave the outmoded, cramped yet familiar semi-comfort of the mother's womb before she embarks down the dark and twisty birth canal. Your dedication will hold you and guide you. It's the slipstream of divine energy summoned by your own will, not just to survive but to thrive in the Being-ness of You.

Let's make one shall we?

Are you dedicated to loving yourself enough to achieve your priorities, independently meeting you needs, taking responsibility for your life and owning your power to choose?

I encourage you to stand for this part. Do so with your feet about hip width apart.

(I recommend you photocopy or photograph and print the following page once you've completed it, and stick it on your wall or bathroom mirror.)

NOW is the moment that the answer to step 2 is placed before us, that there's really only *one decision* to make.

WOULD YOU BE WILLING TO LOVE YOURSELF ENOUGH TO END YOUR PAIN AND SUFFERING?

Do This Now

MY DEDICATION

1. Relax and find your centre of gravity. When you feel ready, take a long, loving surrendered inhale, with a soft open mouth that allows your breath to reach right down to the bottom of your belly, if you can.

2. Place your hands on your heart and say:

"I now ask my Breath; my Life Force, my Creation, to create for me a space of Absolute Love, right Now, all around me and inside of me so that I am completely safe, held and protected in this process of my transformation from here onward. Thank you"

3. Breathe in and receive whatever energy, thoughts or feelings are perceived both in and around you. Welcome pure Divine energy to envelop you. Repeat if need be until you feel safe and protected, but don't over think or analyse it too much. Focus on receiving. Once you feel it we can then cast it forward. When you're ready to do that…

4. Say:

"I Now dedicate this space to my journey of transformation; to release and let go of what no longer serves me and courageously embrace All That I Truly Am for the highest good of myself and therefore all other beings everywhere.

In the name of absolute love, liberation and joy I dedicate myself to (fill in the blank) and commit to living my highest purpose and fulfilling my potential on this planet. Thank you."

5. Enjoy taking full breaths to breathe all those powerfully spoken words in, so that they become part of your cellular matrix.

You Have Now Ignited And Activated Your Hero's Journey!

Hooray!!

Thank you for doing that.

I Love You!

I believe that the decision we need to make is to choose harmony. You don't have to agree with me, of course. Make your own decision.

Loving Reminders

- STEP 2 -

LOVING MYSELF ENOUGH TO MAKE A TRANSFORMATIONAL DECISION

❖ I am a being of free will, therefore, whatever I choose will be so.

❖ I am now willing to love myself enough to make a transformational decision to end my pain and suffering.

❖ Choice is a Power. I either use it or lose it.

❖ I love myself enough to take responsibility for my needs, wants, wellbeing and happiness.

❖ I no longer give my power away by blaming people or situations for not giving me what I need or want.

❖ Taking care of my needs and wants independently is empowering and evolutionary! It includes asking for help and allowing others.

❖ I use my wits and inner wisdom to take care of myself, learning to trust myself first, and therefore knowing when to trust others.

❖ Being conscious in my life is my job.

❖ When I'm stuck it's because I don't know what I don't know and I'm afraid of the unknown, so I need to stop, breathe, and invite 'How'.

❖ Taking responsibility for my life doesn't mean I'm responsible alone for the whole world.

❖ Taking responsibility does mean asking myself what choices could I have made differently to get a different outcome?

❖ When I get stuck in childhood choices and patterns of coping, living from habits and old priorities that no longer serve me, I realise I need to update the records and choose anew from grown-up Me.

❖ What I prioritise gets done.

❖ I understand that Step 1 & 2 go together. They are married. Each breath that comes to me is a point of decision for me to receive life and feel good, or to control, block or close to it and not feel so good. Each breath his a new opportunity where I can make a choice to love myself or not.

❖ I use 'Breathe and Receive' to stay in the present and therefore in my power.

THE FIVE ELEMENTS OF A TRANSFORMATIONAL DECISION ARE:

Own your power

Self-Responsibility

Independently meet your needs

Prioritise

Dedication

True Stories

"Before I met Tara I had not long come out of a relationship in which I felt as if I had totally lost who I was. I needed to find my truth again and discover more of who I was.

I first saw Tara as a one to one client, looking for some clarity and then enrolled on her Year course. This was an incredibly powerful time, as we moved through layers of beliefs that no longer served me and I also began to trust my intuitive senses. I opened up to so much more than I could have imagined. Tara taught me many tools to deal with different aspects that arose, ready to come back into alignment with the truth of who I really am. One of the main tools, and one that I use daily still, Is "I Love You Me."

This very simple yet profound tool is the key to a happy way of living. To really love ourselves is an ever-deepening process, one that I am still enjoying today, nearly 8 years on. I use it when discomfort arises, when forgiveness is needed, I use it in the times when I may feel a little lost or frustrated and I use it on the days when I feel great too, which really helps to amplify how I feel.

Tara greatly encouraged us on the course to speak the words out loud, something that I struggled with at first, now I love to speak it out loud, to allow the words to gently caress my being as well as allowing their vibration to move me from the inside out.

I can now say without a shadow of a doubt that I Love Myself! Really, truly and honestly. What a difference this has made to my life to discover that really I am Love, loving itself!"

—Layla May, UK, Intuitive Energy Healer

Step 3
Acknowledgment

LOVING MYSELF ENOUGH TO ACKNOWLEDGE WHAT'S NOT OK

Sorry, It's All Your Fault.

Here we go, about to enter territory where most people fear to tread; disarmed. Our next bold step is to recognise and properly acknowledge what's wrong, what's not feeling ok, what's been left unhealed and is causing us discomfort and disharmony.

Contrary to popular belief and wishful thinking, attacking our raw, tender and unhealed wounds with positive thinking, pick-me-up affirmations and motivational, butt-kicking fix-it-talk would be like building your beautiful new home on top of a toxic waste dump cleverly disguised with a thick layer of shiny concrete. Imagine that.

Even if your issues are in the past, covered in dust, buried and forgotten; please stop. Take a moment to consider. Ignoring is not the solution.

"The first element of change is awareness.
You can't change something unless you know it exists."
— T. Harv Eker, Secrets of the Millionaire Mind: Mastering the Inner Game of Wealth

Unless you've done this step the ground is not safe, stable and ready for building. Careful excavation and clearing of the ground is absolutely necessary for strong foundation building. Otherwise everything you try to build up in your world is likely to subside or crumble around you, keeping you unfulfilled, dependant and partly broken.

Some of you might prefer to abandon the house and move elsewhere. Why bother with all that hard work? Don't let me deter you, go for it. But, I recommend that you think it through. Can you fool yourself? Can you abandon yourself? Wherever you go your shadow follows. "As above so below" rightly teaches us that whatever appears in our topsoil external reality is a direct mirror of our internal or sub-soil state. Mouldy roots equals rotten tree. A toxic internal environment produces repeatedly negative life experiences.

Self-love requires absolute self-honesty and commitment. Let's discover what haunts us, blocks our future fulfilment and dreams, and what continues to generate lots of what we don't want in our lives. We need to stop and recognise what life is putting in our path for a reason.

"Sorry seems to be the hardest word."
— Sir Elton John

"Look what you've done now!"

"It's all your fault!"

"Say sorry, and act like you mean it!"

"Sorry!!?? You will be!"

When you hear this ominous word 'Sorry', what does it remind you of? Happy memories? I bet 9/10 of us will see ourselves as a small person being yelled at by a bigger person, feeling pretty helpless and intimidated; sort of backed into a corner.

Some might have a sweet remembrance of when someone we loved that hurt or wronged us gave us a tender moment. When they spoke those words "I'm sorry" we felt a sincere connection as if we'd been really seen. Those kinds of moments are rare windows of utter openness. Precious jewels of further unspoken feelings too often get choked back into the throat and swallowed whole. If only they'd had the courage to continue, to bestow you with riches of acknowledgment that you deserve and need.

To the fortunate few, "I'm sorry" is a regular meal deal. It's delivered as part of a package that doesn't stop at the first opening. I'm sorry is an appetiser that whets the pallet of the speaker and is a cue for the listener to stop and allow the ensuing flow of unadulterated vulnerability. It's an exchange starter, but sadly in the vast majority of relationships, intimate and otherwise, we are all half-starved, waiting for somebody to have the guts, and the heart, to meet us at this threshold of emotional nourishment and healing.

A hefty brick of guilt and shame was cast upon us with the word 'sorry' like stones to a criminal at too young an age. We still wear the scars. To speak 'sorry' now would be an admission of guilt, an apology for the 'fault' we apparently caused, and too heavy a weight of responsibility to bear for the inner child who didn't understand the grown up world he'd become embroiled in. Better stick to the old faithful "It wasn't me, I didn't do it" and shift the blame, redirect attention, anything but bear the brunt of an adult's scorn.

The lack of 'sorrys' can stockpile. The many times when someone ought to, should have, said sorry to us and taken responsibility for the awful thing that happened, acknowledging our hurt, stack up like a pile of old stories waiting for an opportune time when somebody wants to hear them. For some of us, these often sour and bitter tales are like well read books, covers threadbare with the telling and re-telling of our version. It eases our pain none, just cements it in deeper as part of the fabric of our bodily home. For others, they remain in the back closet gathering dust. Forgotten but not forgiven, waiting like ghosts in the cupboard for the right time to jump out and have their day of retribution. For others the mildewed resentments sicken them. A dank pile of rotten feelings cause such a stench that the throat, clenched, tries to avoid the spilling admittance of such sadness and dark betrayal. It lingers like the stink of damp.

Everybody has a pile of unsaid 'sorrys,' either from them or to them, or both: Mostly both.

A gut full, if the truth be known. Often it's not until we are brought to our knees in sheer desperation and heart wrenching need for confession that the coffers crack, the stack folds and all the hidden dragons come out. This is on a good day. How many people take a bellyful of resentments to their grave, never able to give in to the humility needed to grant their liberation?

Those Three Little Words

What's so wrong with saying, "I am sorry"? Why are these little 3 words harder to say than the other 3 hardest words to say? Is it because there's more than just one sorry that we need to hear or say? In which case the whole book gets stuck in our throat or blocked by the ironclad heart. And, once you've opened that door there's a monster of a pile, causing a froth of swirling bile, deeper down in the bowels of the raging, spitting beast within you! That sleeping old tiger, resentment, is a bitter and unhandsome thing to release, and is best left lying — right?

Well, not if you want to be healthy and happy, no. Not if you want to be close to people, enjoy intimate relationships with partners, lovers, parents and children. But if your pride has become a hardened second skin, and the reconciling too much face to lose, then the unresolved beast has already become bigger than you. It has over-powered you, scared you off and intimidated you into silent suffering. You've made your choice, so live with it you must. I can tell you now it's like unattended damp creeping from the basement and up into your living room. It will spread, and the decay will be prolific. Untreated resentment is a killer.

What's the solution then?

Well, my friend, make a choice. Are you worth redeeming? Are you worth saving? Is the little child in you still breathing enough to be resuscitated and reclaimed and released from the burdens that ail her or him? If no-one has been willing to be the much needed grown up in your life to come get you, hold you, and un-tap the barrel of nectar-like 'sorrys' to your thirsty ears, then the hero of the day has to be you.

You must now love yourself enough to be your own grown up, to be your own hero and to be your own saviour.

That resentment could be maturing nicely in your emotional cellar for some time to come. What are you saving it for? Surely if someone else was going to take responsibility for your pain they would have done it by now? You can't afford to keep waiting indefinitely and it's not fair on you to wait any longer.

The True Beauty Of Sorry

'Sorry' has an original meaning that, like many a beautiful and holy thing, has been savaged by the ages. Its original purity has been pillaged, leaving only tattered remnants that do not do it full justice. The scraps we use are un-whole and leave empty gaps in their meaning, allowing bugs to creep in and make their nest.

To say Sorry, is actually the MOST beautiful way of acknowledging what has moved out of harmony. Like a dissonant note in an orchestra of life, something needs to be first heard, then spoken of or acknowledged, adjusted and brought back into harmony for the over-all good of the symphony being played. There's been an err in the path of justice, a fault in the Divine Order of creation. A note that was missed, a step misplaced, a moment of unconsciousness or hesitation that got us lost suddenly. Something happened to bring a cloud over our sky and block out the sunlight and warmth. Was it OUR fault? Did WE do it?

When you consider there's a billion other possible game plays and a gazillion other possible contributing factors: the placement of the stars that night; the direction of the wind and the unexpected arrival of an unwelcome guest; is it FAIR that we bear the full brunt of the blame?

Now, life does not happen in black and white; Blaming, guilt loading, shifting weight between us as we strive for a fair game, or to win and conquer all. 'It's him, not me' kind of attitude doesn't cut the mustard these days. Ultimately, not saying 'sorry' is a refusal to take responsibility, the symptoms of which are:

Powerlessness; an inflated, justified and unbalanced sense of self that lives in constant contradiction with the world around oneself; perpetual anger, frustration, resentment, meanness, spiteful words, hardness of face and a resolve to prove oneself, sadness, depression, lethargy, pointlessness, disconnection, 'whatever — I ain't boverred' kind of attitude, denial, followed by denial of denial, coldness, indifference, and did I mention powerlessness? It is self-preservation at all costs, and false, unearned PRIDE.

The masks are wearing thin these days, so, many people with any kind of awareness can see straight through the defences of a person loaded with un-eased pain. We can also see straight through people who wear their pain like a medal, unready to give it up and walk in comfort and instead act the martyr in their righteous suffering, that's also 'Old-school'. Whilst we can appreciate the great souls in history who sacrificed their lives and suffered for the apparent benefit of the rest of us, it's really only fair to ask ourselves *Did it actually work?*

NO, BEFORE YOU REACT IN DEFENCE, BE HONEST.

Let us look at the soldiers who gave their lives, the nuns who renounced theirs, the Gandhi's and Martin Luther King's of the world. Whilst in their time they did what they could, and what felt right given the knowledge and resources that were available then, they did an incredible service. They were history makers and game changers. Let us honour their lives and contributions. But, let us also learn from their experiences, not keep repeating them and wasting life.

What good did it do *them* and is it REALLY necessary to sacrifice ourselves in this modern day and age to make a difference? I believe not. I believe there's another option, one that's more empowering, less self-destructive, and more of an example that *everyone* can follow - to their own, and all of our mutual benefit. It's a way that works as a win-win-win situation; a duplicatable, more sustainable solution. With the greatest respect, not everyone wants to, or is able to, carry a cross for the sake of humanity.

So how can we make a difference, impact positive transformation and Be the change we seek in the world?

"I'm Sorry, Me"

Try saying that without feeling guilty, or an immediate resistance and involuntary reaction to spit the words back out, or throw up. Or, maybe those words have got no further than your brain and are being chewed to pieces right now. "Sorry for **what?**"

Take a deep breath. We need to prepare the soil before we plant seeds, and we need to prepare you to receive. Like almost everyone, you have probably become defensive, guarded, and suspicious and pretend not to need any charitable acts of kindness. You have a voice in your head that you are used to listening to that beats you up all day, long, (for your own good and protection you imagine).

This voice says things like "I don't need anyone to say sorry to me. I'm over it, *I'm fine* now"

That know-it-all voice will probably also say thing like "I know I **should** be kinder to myself....I **should** stop giving myself a hard time, I **should** stop eating so much junk, I **should** go to the gym more, I **should** be nicer to my other/kids/husband, *I should I should I should...*

Stop, enough. Take a deep breath. I don't believe in being cruel to be kind. It's more like shooting yourself in the foot by "should"-ing and forcing yourself to do things that your heart, higher mind and body don't want to do just yet. Tony Robbins often says,

"Stop shoulding all over yourself."
— Tony Robbins, Life Coach and NLP Founder

I think you get the idea.

Try This:

"I'm sorry me, that I am sometimes/frequently/constantly putting you down, and telling you what you should be, rather than loving you just how you are"

Or

"I'm sorry me that you think you don't need to say sorry because you don't know what for and it doesn't make sense, but maybe a part of You, Me, needs to hear this"

And

"I'm sorry me that even though you try really hard and do really well, you don't feel quite right"

Take a deep breath. With your mouth open this time, and your jaw and throat relaxed and soft like a baby. You can't swallow your self-love medicine if you're tightly clenched, controlling and stubborn about it!

Let the words trickle down, soften, relax. Breathe. They will find their way to the parts of you that REALLY NEED to hear that. Like watering a plant. The flowers may look *'fine'* but the roots are parched. Let the water of your self-serving kindness soak in and feed the roots of your flower.

Do This Now

How do you feel right now? What's the most prominent, in your face thing that's upsetting you? Say it out loud now.

Take a deep breath and again say out loud "I'm sorry me that you feel....................."

Resist the temptation to add extra words like "you'll be alright...don't worry" etc etc... Don't smother the truth of your feelings with sticking plaster affirmations and fix it tape!

Breathe. Let your FEELINGS BREATHE. They've been underground behind closed doors and thick walls for too long already.

Poor you suffocating in the darkness!

I am sorry poor little you that you keep being unacknowledged and managed instead of heard...

Saying Sorry Is Not Being Pathetic

'Sorry' can be like Turrets Syndrome, afflicting people who suffer from chronic un-recognition. The lack of attention they receive causes countless, uncontrollable sorrys to fall from their mouths and drop like dead flies from a decaying self-esteem. It's an excruciating disease, ravaging the victim with the impulse to apologise for just about everything, especially *existing*, as if **they** are the cause of the problem, the one in the way, the one who faltered and failed and shouldn't even be here. It's not yourself you should be apologising for, but *it is* you who deserves an apology. You need to be recognised, without apology, to validate and strengthen you.

How To Acknowledge The Unacknowledged Parts

Saying sorry is a conversation opening. If it's opened your flood gates and got you scared that a back-log will uncontrollably spill all over the place, and make a mess, and make you look stupid, and ruin your make up or your nicely arranged presentation face, then I AM sorry. Sorry to see you so upset, and hurt inside.

Maybe it just makes you plain angry and you don't want to say it.

Maybe you want to throw this book away already. I'm sorry you feel angry. Maybe no-one's heard you before and you need a lot of sorrys to make up for the damage that was done. I'm sorry.

Maybe you've numbed out and you're reading this as if it's happening to someone else and not you. Who are you trying to read this book for? I'm sorry you think it's not for you, that you don't need the healing, that your 'someone else' does and you want to help them more than help yourself because it's easier than facing your own pain and dealing with it. I'm sorry.

Maybe you're all healed, and nothing in you needs to hear or say sorry because you're enlightened and perfect. Hello enlightened and perfect you! What are you reading this book for then? I'm sorry you think all your healing is done and you don't need it either. You're probably reading this so you can help other people and maybe change the world and make it a better place so that you can feel better in some way. I'm sorry that I'm asking you to say, "I'm sorry me" and you don't even know what you need it for, but it's bringing up your emotions.

I love you.

Phew!

Thank you for bearing with me. You see how many ways we have of avoiding and keeping face? That was just a few. Trust me, I still say sorry to myself regularly. It doesn't stop. This is a habit you can practice for life. Like cleaning your home. You don't get a good cleaner in once a year to give it a couple of hours cleaning, just like you don't take a life-times worth of stuff to a therapist once or twice and expect to come out clean and shiny and new. It's a once a week clean up, minimum. And then, there's all the little bits that you have to tidy away and clear up as you go along so that your kitchen or bathroom doesn't become unbearable and disgusting. Then there's the clearing and cleaning of certain places that you wouldn't invite the cleaner to do, it's your job and yours alone. You can be your own cleaner AND you can get help. It's all good.

Maybe you're the kind of person who cleans obsessively and still nothing's quite right and feeling good? I'm sorry. Maybe you've had a ton of therapy too, but you're still not right. I'm sorry. Maybe you're the kind of person who has never learned to clean or tidy up after yourself, maybe you've always had a maid or a mother or a father to do it for you. I am sorry. It's time to clean you. Because if you have avoided it so far, doing everything else but taking up the mop of self-love and splurging it into all your dirtiest, darkest corners, then my friend, my love, You are missing out on a very satisfying feeling of self-empowerment. The satisfaction that You did it for You. That you can stand on your own two feet and really take responsibility for your own inner and outer environment. That you are NOT helpless, you are powerful and capable beyond measure but you are letting yourself down in certain areas that need your attention. Take a deep breath my friend. Do you want to arise and shine and reclaim your authentic power and right to be fully and totally, independently, exactly Yourself? Do you owe it to yourself? Not to show **them,** or prove to anyone else what you're made of. Not for retribution and retaliation, but for Self Love and Self respect and Liberation from whatever it is that has you chained and pained in your life right now. Want to get to work?

Without effort, let yourself be breathed. Let the great cleaner and cleanser of breath, like the ocean, wash in, and up, upon your inner-shores. And when you think it can't reach any further, any deeper, it does. That little foamy white edge of ocean that licks up and gets your feet wet...surrender to it. Get wet. All the way in and down to where the tide of great kindness and relief needs to reach.

Have you let go a little?

Do This Now

See what happens when you say these sentences out loud, with your hand on your heart.

- *"I'm sorry Me, for having avoided taking good and proper care of You so far"*

- *"I'm sorry Me that I thought it was someone else's job and I've been waiting, wishing and   wanting others to get their act together so that they would finally take care of you, Me"*

- *"I'm sorry Me that meanwhile, no-one was really looking out for you, seeing you,   understanding you and loving you in just the way you need it. You've been alone all this   time. I'm so sorry Me. I really see you now. I feel you. I get it. I'm sorry."*

And iiiiiiiiin with the soft, sweeping, bottom-of-the-belly, relaxed throat kind of breath.... Aaaaaaand ahhhhhh.... let it go.

Anything else you want to clear and get off your chest right now? Go for it.

"I'm sorry me that you feel _____ and you need _____   and it's not fair because _____. I hear you, me. I'm so sorry"

Feeling a bit better?

Well done, You!

Now, when you really want to take up this mantle and transform your world, or you just want to see what other strangely effective things I'm going to lovingly encourage you to do, go to the next chapter.

But first, let's go do your homework.

> **Go to the Step 3 section in your workbook and complete Exercise 1.**
>
> **It'll make you feel properly acknowledged**
>
> **~ Thank you!**

Saying Sorry To Others

Is it hard for you to say sorry to someone else, or does it still feel bad or uncomfortable when you do? Why should you apologise when they are the one who did wrong to you? Why should you apologise when you didn't do anything wrong?

That's where we have to stop, breathe and remember not to jump into the victim mode again. That's where we have to become extra conscious and decide to love ourselves enough to clear our self of all negative attachments to pain, no matter who or where we think they might have come from. Continuing to believe that it's someone else's fault and shirking responsibility for how you feel, will keep you small, suffering and in pain. It's humbling I know, and sometimes too much, as if saying sorry means you're stooping to their low level, or bowing in front of them in submission. That doesn't feel empowering at all and will likely have you closing the book right now if that's what you continue to choose to believe.

I'm sorry that you don't want to say sorry. I'm sorry that saying sorry makes you feel bad, or angry and defensive, or justified and proud. Perhaps even arrogant and hard.

But, ultimately it's an empowering act of compassion to acknowledge where we've shifted the blame for our pain to someone else, and let ourselves become the victim of their behaviour. There's also a possibility that we see some of the picture clearly but not the whole, in which case our limited perspective prevents us from seeing the case accurately at all. Take a breath. Despite first appearances, that's actually true. I can't help you unless you want to help yourself.

Always Come Back And Start With Yourself

Acknowledging disharmony in your life is as important as acknowledging that the fire-alarm is going off in your house. It is simply not safe or wise to ignore it.

Have you got a constant alarm bell of disharmony ringing in the background of your life?

The problem with acknowledging the problem is that it's frightening. All too often we have no clue what to do with the disharmony once it's been acknowledged. We avoid looking our demons in the eye for fear of being burned alive by them, or for fear of seeing something wrong or shameful about ourselves, that's why we avoid it. It's not necessarily the case. Saying sorry doesn't make you feel ashamed or wrong when you do it right. Saying sorry makes you feel better. Saying Sorry makes you brave.

Loving Reminders

-STEP 3-

I LOVE MYSELF ENOUGH TO SAY SORRY TO MY PAIN.

❖ I lovingly acknowledge what's out of harmony in me by saying "Sorry" to it.

❖ Saying "Sorry" means "I see you, I hear you, I feel you and I accept you, Me," and more.

❖ Saying 'Sorry' to myself is the most perfect and beautifully empowering way to acknowledge what doesn't feel right and what isn't in harmony.

❖ Saying "I'm Sorry Me" means I love myself enough to validate my own pain and open a healing conversation.

❖ Speaking directly to the heart of the wound is the most potent way I can begin to heal anything.

❖ Sorry is not an admission of guilt, shame, wrong, fault or that I am bad.

❖ Saying 'Sorry' to someone else means that I lovingly acknowledge and validate their pain. It does not imply that I accept blame.

❖ Saying sorry means I am open and true. I have the courage to be fully honest and say what's really going on, without avoiding, hiding or denying.

❖ Speaking honestly, with love, sincerity and humility is empowering. It strengthens me in my core.

❖ Choosing to say 'Sorry' to all disharmony that I experience in me and my world means I am taking responsibility for my life, and it makes a difference in the world.

❖ Saying "sorry me," is the kindest thing to say when I am hurting, especially when it's the hardest thing to do.

❖ I am worth saying sorry to. Every part of me deserves to hear it.

❖ Acknowledgment and validation is a need. I love myself enough to meet my own need.

❖ Acknowledgement brings instant clarity and relief to any situation.

True Stories

"Over the last three decades I've experienced a wide variety of healing modalities which were all beneficial however, Tara Love Perry's 'I love you, Me' method was the most profound inner process I have ever experienced...Her uncanny intuition brought me into a place in my heart where old pain was hidden away and she taught me how to let it go once and for all... I was so surprised that I had been carrying it around for all these years and I felt a deep sense of relief to finally acknowledge the truth of it and let it go...

Instead of just giving you information or guidance about your emotional life, she gently brings you into your own heart where the beauty of your inner child is awaiting you...In my opinion, the most needed healing work on the planet is learning to love our wounded inner child who is the key to our joy & creativity in life...I love you, Me, is a fast track method for learning to nurture and protect your inner child, which will make a profound difference in the quality of your life...Tara Love is a powerful guide who gently teaches us how to embrace our tender most feelings while we learn how to nurture, protect and support the most vulnerable parts of our inner being...I am deeply grateful to Tara for the Wisdom, Light and Love which she brings to her work as the Champion of our Inner Children..."

—Des Coroy - USA, Author of '21st Century Relationship Guide'

"I've benefited from Tara's technique in ways too profound to articulate. I try to remember to use the "I love you, me" method when I have feelings I desperately want to disown. It makes me pause and acknowledge and accept the feeling or thought rather than trying to escape it. I sometimes find I'm guided to use this technique when I work with others; it helps to deepen my compassion, and my clients benefit from having their unmentionable thoughts and feelings named without shame."

—Vanessa Arnold, Dubai. Holotropic breath work facilitator and healer

Step 4
True Release

LOVING MYSELF ENOUGH
TO LET GO ENTIRELY

"Let It Go Already"

Grrr! How annoying is that phrase!?

"Let it GO."

Let it go **where?**

What exactly am I letting go of?

And, Why **Should I** let it go?

Oooh, it makes my blood boil!

Do you ever feel like that?

Letting go is part of the puzzle to releasing and restoring our youthfulness, happiness and dignity. However, these words are frequently spoken to serve as a stiff shot of self-preservation with a quick sweep under the rug of something we don't want to deal with, instead of a genuine release. How does that really work for you?

Wouldn't you rather have the actual experience of relief and relinquish? Could you raise your right hand, and with the left hand on Your Heart, say honestly to yourself:

"I have well and truly 'let go' of all the things I believe I've let go of, because nothing in me, whatsoever, feels any sense of pain, bitterness, anger, vengefulness, resentment, hardness, sadness, denial or protective covering about it now, and I have absolutely NO expectations, wishes or secret needs waiting to be fulfilled, because I did so well in letting it go already."

Say that aloud and see how it feels. It's very different out of your mouth than it is in your head. Is your jaw clenched and tight? How's your throat? Soft and yielded, or constricted and suffocated like a hanged man? Have you got a tender little lump of well-earned pride stuck in your throat?

B~R~E~A~T~H~E.

Are you attached to, or attracted to, the **belief** that you've let it go, because it gives you some sense of security? Does it give you a sense of distance from the painful thing or person that you wanted to let go of? It's easier to believe that we've let something painful go, even if we haven't, rather than to feel the horrible, helpless, stuck-ness of our attachment to something we want to be rid of. It's like 'letting go' of litter to the floor of your house. It's not gone, it's just not being carried around with you anymore. You will still see it lying there, but you will try to ignore it and blank it out, pretending you don't see it. But, the litter will remain. How many 'let-it-go's are cluttering your floor? You know how many by how stuck, ill or tired you are in your life, and how many times you keep tripping over the same situation again and again, only the labels have changed. How long is it going to be before your living environment becomes unbearable, and you're swimming up to your neck in the sewerage of your unresolved debris whilst screaming, "I've had I up to Here!" (hand to cut-throat position), overwhelmed by trash?

Letting it go is a process. If you've done your work right and all the other pieces are in place, your letting it go will have worked out well for you and you'll be merrily, merrily, merrily, merrily floating down the dreamy river of life, all in flow, happy, healthy and aglow.

On its own, 'letting it go' it's a poor man's substitute for giving yourself the relief and freedom from pain and suffering you really deserve.

Yes, the relief and freedom you really deserve.

If it's true, or you want it to be true, that you really deserve freedom and relief from pain, suffering, being overwhelmed, staying afloat, keeping your head above water, and from feeling deep-down 'Not Okay', then please say out loud, with your hand on your heart ~

"I am really sorry Me, that even though you did really well trying to let (........ fill in the blank until it's all spoken out and you can breathe again) go, you actually still don't feel totally OK. I'm sorry Me, that you deserve to have real freedom and relief from your pain and suffering, and maybe I didn't know How before, or I wasn't ready, but I am Now. I'm

sorry Me, that You haven't had true freedom and total relief in your life just yet."

Relax, you're in process right now. Did that feel good?

Now actually say it out loud and not just in your head...

Release ~ Making The Choice

True relief feels like when you've climbed to the top of Kilimanjaro with a 80 kilo pack on your back and then someone takes it off you.

True relief is when the armour you've worn into battle for the past 20 years gets thrown on a fire and melted down to pure and simple metal again, all tarnishes burned clean and your scars healed.

True relief is when you've been out for the first night since your beautiful, brand new first baby is born, and you finally get home, take her from the babysitter and have her back in your safe arms where she belongs.

Relief is when you've buried your dead with love, gratitude, forgiveness, honour and rightful acknowledgment for all that they were in life, and will still be after death.

Relief is when you're empty of pain, not just empty.

Now come back to step 1 and step 2

Breathe

Receive

Make a decision...What is it that you'd really like to 'let go' of?

What do you want true freedom from, for good, forever, in your life?

Choose Now.

> **Please go to Step 4 Exercise 1 in your workbook.**
>
> **~ Thank you!**

Real-Ease Me

So, what is the Big Secret that now makes your new decision to let stuff go, possible?

How are you going to do it? Well, guess what, you're already doing it! It's now possible because you decided it is. Before, you couldn't see another way forward that would work for you, so you stuck with being stuck. Now you really are ready to let go... well more than you were before anyway. You might find that you keep having to make new decisions as you progress, because now that you are focused on you, and **You** have your attention, it's highly likely and very probable that you are going to see things in a new and fascinating light. You are going to have to be really kind to yourself as you realise a whole load of things that you've been doing, believing and carrying around on your back like a martyr, that have stopped you from being the You of your dreams. Bless you. I love you. It's ok, we all do it. We're all in the changing room together, so you're not alone.

Take a deep breath again. Notice how much you hold in just by holding your breath all the time. It's as if you try to stop having the weird, uncomfortable and sometimes horrible feelings that my words are bringing up for you by not breathing.

Breathe Easy

If you keep taking deep breaths and breathe **all** of the words in, like allowing raindrops to soak into your soil, they will wash through that sticky layer of discordance and discomfort and begin to cleanse it through. The energy will move. You will begin to feel less uncomfortable and more enlightened; lighter, freer and at ease. If my words aren't relevant to you, they will wash straight through and help feed the ground where your ancestors lay and wash them clean too. Just keep breathing and receiving and getting used to allowing feelings and allowing my words instead of resisting and blocking them.

Perhaps you hold your breath and stay tight because you think what I'm saying doesn't apply to you, or that you have better ideas? You won't know what's really true until you can feel it. Your mind doesn't have all the answers you know. It's not the master intelligence in our human system, it's actually very limited and only part of our internal navigation system. What you resist persists, so just keep letting the breath flow deeper so the 'inner you' comes back to life. *How can you relate to Yourself if you can't feel yourself?*

Breathe. It's all good.

You've had a contract of sorts going on, with a part of yourself, with a feeling, with a belief, or with a person. Now you are letting it go, freeing yourself from the contract and returning what you only borrowed, or leased, in the first place.

It's easy to forget that even our bodies are borrowed. They are ours for a while and then even they have to be returned to the leaser, Mother Earth. All agreements here are temporary. All of it has a shelf life, a due by date. None of what we call 'real' has indefinite sustainability. This breath is borrowed, we have to give that back too. Our thoughts are borrowed, we can give back the ones that we don't enjoy.

When I ask people what they want to achieve for themselves or what they want to be free from, "How?" raises it's big, ugly head of impending impossibility every time. It's the same when I tell them that they can have, be, do anything their heart desires, or ask them 'so, what is your wish?'

An exasperated, 'But How??!' arrives before the 'Yes please I'll take my joy, freedom and abundant, new reality thank you very much!"

So, here we go...how DO we release our pain, stop fighting, drop the armour, quit trying, take the weight off, stop carrying our baggage, bury our dead, hold our baby and find that long sought after relief?

"Please Forgive Me, Me"

Forgiveness is THE most beautiful and perfect way to release what no longer serves us.

It's a sweet fragrance that breezes through the sour stench of bitterness; a cooling balm for angry shame, and a clear-water spring for deep buried grief to arise and be reborn as relief.

True forgiveness is when we are able to give back what was never really ours to keep. Would you be willing to release yourself from your pain and suffering and anything that aggrieves or limits you from being your ultimate, glowing and glorious self, simply because you NEED it? Would your life be better for it?

On your next 'in' breath, receive the force that animates you, feel and relax.

Please forgive me that Life has been a hard road for you; that you have walked with stones in your shoes for many years. Please forgive me that maybe there are few, or none, who truly understand your pain as you do, and finding a way to release has been hard or near impossible. Please forgive me if you feel defensive, protective or angry and don't want to forgive ANYONE because it feels like admitting your guilt or letting someone off the hook.

Please forgive me that even though you've been really good, loving and kind, forgiving even, but you still feel wounded to your core and burdened in your soul.

I love you, I'm sorry.

And I can ask you to finally, truly release what no longer serves you.... but until **you** decide to do it for yourself; you being the one who TOTALLY gets how it all feels, and you being the one who can best empathise with yourself; then you will still carry your pain around like a medal to validate your injustices and injuries.

For all that ails you, and for your own sake, now choose to release and say - "Please forgive me, ME." Yes, you've got it - OUT LOUD; for You.

Now swallow that medicine. With a big, open, soft breath IN let the words trickle down your throat and find the place that needs soothing.

Forgiveness Is The Key

To ask forgiveness is not a new, new-age thing. Nor is it a religious thing. The word itself acts like a key that literally unlocks pain and releases it. When you apply this key to yourself you are giving yourself permission to heal and be free. If you are waiting for someone else's permission, please forgive me but you might not get it. Just as someone else who perhaps awaits your permission to heal by your admission as the one responsible for their pain or problem, may also not get it from you.

Are we going to go round and round on the merry go round of liability, waiting for the person in front to turn around and see us, chasing our tail, chasing someone else's tail, needing their permission to be free and happy?

Forgiveness Is Your Liberation

You do it for your own purposes, because if you're not free how can you fully live? If the state of your wellbeing is tied to someone else because you need something from them, or **don't need it** (whilst you're quietly seething inside) then you are not free. Neither are they. Is it worth continuing in this way, making both of you bound in chains of fateful misery? If you're happiness is dependent upon someone being a certain way, or your life situation being a certain way, or the world being a certain way, then you are not free. You are hopelessly bound, and strangled probably, by ropes of dependency, expectancy and desperate disappointment. The noose is round your neck. You become stagnant. The situation perpetuates. It will have to be you who decides to cut your own neck free, which might feel like letting all those *'others'* off the hook. It might feel like letting the bastards win! It might feel like you have given up the fight.

Yes. You will have to stop fighting and decide if you are ready for peace; within You.

Forgiveness is totally selfish; an enlightened selfishness. We have to apply our knowledge, faith, love, compassion, understanding, blessings and best co-operation possible to our own selves. Why? Because when we know what works and what doesn't work, we become the proof of the pudding, so to speak. Then we can walk with integrity and not be the hypocrite that we all love to hate. Then can we be the master of our own life's fate instead of relying on other Masters, Mothers, Gods or Gurus to do the work for us. They have a life too you know....

Live, learn, grow, let go, stop being dependant. Time to stand on your own two feet.

Forgive Me For What?! I Didn't Do Anything!

The thought of having to ask someone else's forgiveness can be terrifying. It can bring a huge amount of resistance, a lump in the throat and a foreboding incitement of guilt and shame. It's not that asking for forgiveness is in itself bad, but the ensuing toxicity due to the way in which this word has been used historically is enough to make anyone purse their lips tight and pointblank refuse to swallow.

Before I properly understood the true meaning of forgiveness, what used to pop into my head was a movie image of a catholic confession box, dark, musty and eerily intimidating, where small children have to confess **something,** even if they didn't want to, or think that they particularly needed to. I've heard stories where people have invented a sin to confess because it was expected that they had sinned. 'God's' Judgement upon them would be worse if they didn't confess to anything. These were people raised in the belief 'You are born a sinner and you will die a sinner,' unless the sins are confessed and repented for appropriately.

Which is worse, confessing your sins to a veiled, mysterious or invisible character with the power to preside judgment over your life after death? Or, not confessing to anything because you don't think you've done anything wrong, but have to live in quiet fear that a larger than life, omnipotent eye sees your every move, and who will one day find you and make you pay for things you can't remember doing, or didn't do? The fear of either, or both, can keep you running round and round in emotional circles, getting tied up in knots trying to find a way to wriggle out of the whole ordeal.

I imagine, like many children, you learned that asking for forgiveness is a clear admission of your guilt. You're effectively admitting that you are faulted, imperfect or have bad things on your conscience to which you should confess. It's shaming where shaming isn't due.

Have you had an experience like this when you were small? How did it feel to have to 'own up' to something that offended someone else in such a way as to incur his or her wrath and disapproval? How many of us, even now as adults, spend our precious time enduring the inner torture of self-justifying mental monologues with ourselves, convincing ourselves that it wasn't our fault, that we are innocent, that we didn't know any better and we couldn't help it?

Run away! It wasn't me! I didn't do it! Agghhhhh!

For some of us, (I hope) the prospect of forgiveness is not **all that** heavy. But, when confronted by our partner, boss or parent, demanding that we admit a fault, or own-up to being the cause of **their** anger, pain, grief etc, it can be every bit as tormenting and painful. How do we respond? Is it possible that we inadvertently revert to that little kid we used to be, torn by the nightmare of either:

1.   Admitting our 'bad' to appease the unhappy grown up, despite the terrifying consequences, even if the 'own-up' is a lie?

2.   Denying everything, pleading our innocence and doing a runner to shake off the evil scent of blame, then having to live with the secret stench of guilt hovering over our conscience; did we do bad or didn't we? Was it really our fault??

This is a hellish conflict between our emotional responses, need for survival and sense of justice or truth.

Phew. Take a deep breath. Remembering can feel intense. Even if you have no conscious memories surfacing, notice what your throat is doing right now. How clenched or relaxed your jaw feels. Has your chest turned to stone? Perhaps you feel a headache coming on...

It's okay. You are safe right now. I'm not judging you.

If you can hear a judge judging you it's probably the one in your head. The one that's been gaining power as you get older. This judge exists because of the seeds that were planted in your head when you were small about being at fault, and about what was wrong and what was right. And, if you can hear the judge and inner critic, you can probably also detect a little-you voice saying "It's not fair! I don't like this, go away..."

So how do we get out of this?

Forgive Me While I Rant...

What if true forgiveness has nothing to do with being wronged, being lesser than or subservient to some higher authority, nor a shameful, painful admission of sin or guilt, but a way to release, restore and make whole <u>something which doesn't feel so good?</u>

What if we could take a special kind of cleaning cloth and rub away what isn't really true and polish you up until you're shining again, like the Golden Buddha story?

Personally, and forgive me while I rant...I do not believe in condemnation and judgment by God or a God figure that rules us and to whom we must obey. It just doesn't make rational or emotional sense to me that such a thing exists. But, it excellently explains why so many people are still suffering in this world due to indoctrinated beliefs that human beings are low-life devil's spawn, destined to go to hell unless we repent for our sins and be good, god abiding citizens forever and ever amen (or versions thereof).

God is not a big brother bully. The belief that a being like that exists, with the power to condemn me to hell if I don't appease him - IS enough to put the fear of God in me, and the fear of living, AND the fear of dying. It would probably cause me to feel enslaved, entrapped, punished, judged, not good enough, not godly enough, and consistently paranoid and unhappy. What if that kind of God or deity isn't real, but is instead a made-up character, a story of something that was embedded in us to believe and control us by, throughout history, for literally Ages? What if **that** kind of 'God' is only alive and ever so supremely powerful in our imaginations because of the stories we were told as children, like the bogie monster?

Just, what if???

How would that feel?

I'm am definitely not trying to convert or distort anyone's sacred or religious beliefs, but I do encourage you to think and feel about it for a moment.

Do we have to **believe** in a deity or God of some sort so that we exist? Do we have to ask, repent or even be grateful for our breath for it to continue coming to us? Do we need to have Faith to wake up in the morning?

I don't think so.

Forgiveness From God

I don't have to **believe** in a deity to exist, *do I?*

I exist and you exist and we exist, right now, breath by breath, because we are designed to do so. Could it be that we are GIVEN this life as a gift, as an opportunity for nature and the force of Creation, whatever *that is,* to create for its own sake and exist AS us?

Does the flower have to worship the sun because she's a lowly earthly being, for without the light she would not exist? Therefore, must she spend her days forever after repenting because the sun gave her life?

Or is she simply drawn, intuitively, naturally, towards turning her petal face to the light because it feels good and nourishes her, inspiring her to grow? And what if she didn't? Would the sun punish her? Clouds come, storms come. The flower still grows.

Are moles, and badgers and nocturnal, burrowing creatures punished for not basking in the sun and praising him? Are they lower and less than the sparrows and the skylarks? Do we think that because trees die and our compost pile rots that there is an evil in the world, and that death is a monster to be feared? We can see from our garden roses that compost/ rotten, decayed matter/ death and darkness, makes them bloom ever more beautifully.

Nature is innocent is it not? So, why do we perceive nature as innocent, and yet not ourselves? Are we so separate from nature, including the sun and the stars of the dark, night sky, so different? Are we exempt from the same laws that create harmony and order in the plant and animal kingdom?

Ask yourself if you would wish your beloved, pure innocent child to grow up with the same torturing beliefs that you do, and to be governed so cruelly by them as you are? If you were God, what kind of world would you give to your children? I'm sure that as a loving parent, you would want them to have a free, happy and love filled life, with as little drama and pain as possible, but everything for them to learn what's right for them and what's not; to teach them, and guide them in life, that they may grow to be strong, unique, respectful, valuable, contributing, happy and free individuals. Would you not?

You would want for them the very best, everything that you yourself did not have, so that they may not suffer as you have. You are a beautiful person, an amazing parent. Your life wasn't perfect and yet you want perfection for your child, and you would strive to give it to them as best you could. And yet, why do we think that we are condemned and forced to suffer, and that **we** have no other choice? People say, "Hey ho, that's life" when something doesn't go our way. It's not the Universe or God that gives us bad days, it's we who do it to ourselves, because we don't realise the amazing, great responsibility we have to direct a part of Creation; and that part of Creation is your 'Me'.

Spirituality is straight forward, and not this big mystery that it's been veiled as. The truth will set you free, and the truth is yours to own and for you to know.

It's my observation and experience that Life just IS. It moves, shapes, moves again and dismantles... always creating and expressing itself through form and colour, texture and shape, sound and vibrations. Life is supreme intelligence that gives all of creation an instinct for Home, with unique navigational homing instruments included. All that lives has the tools needed to survive and thrive and find its way home. Life is humble, like water, it bends and flows and becomes very pliable to our will.

There Are Boundaries

Life also has boundaries. Once we break the boundaries of life, which means to sever contact with the heart and essence of it, fail to trust it and go against its natural flow, we become out of synch. We become like a limb severed, a branch cut, a stream blocked from entering the great river, or a child lost, bewildered and alone. Our life energy will cease to flow when we disengage from the greater force, body and presence of Life itself. It stands to reason that our physicality would wilt in such conditions, that damp and decay would slowly set in, that death would surely start to reclaim us and turn us back to compost. The stream would dry up if it were severed from the river, or turn mouldy, become infested, stagnant and smelly. The branch would eventually rot and return to the earth. The child, lost and detached from her parents would not be able to cease her crying, struggle endlessly to find her way home alone, or give up home to live in her abandoned state.

When we are disconnected from the flow of life because of rocks and boulders of pain in our river, we are incapable of reproducing life under life's natural laws. When we cease to trust life we ironically also fear the loss of it too, and do anything possible, even unnatural interventions to prevent death's grip from snatching us back to the soil from whence we came.

The only thing that severs our connection with Life is a ruling belief that we are separate from the beauty and simplicity, the obvious natural, and exquisite perfection of it.

If we believe in a judgemental higher authority who controls or disallows us the freedom to be exactly who we are defaulted to be — innocent, wise, wonderfully creative, child-like beings, with an inclination towards happiness and harmony, then we are immediately f***ed! We cross a safety boundary that Life set for us.

I experience a very real presence of unconditional love in my life. I sometimes call this energy God; it feels good. There is no judgment, because that's what unconditional means: Without condition. There is only love, the kind of love which I want to learn from, and aspire to be fully conscious of at all times. It is always there; ever present, like the sun; like my breath, like creation. If I have a higher Authority that governs my life, this is it. Love. It's not separate from me, nor is it controlling or dictating to me; merely humbly, brightly, present and continuously giving. Love is busy being Me. And it wants me to recognise it.

Often, other 'Higher Authorities' loom overhead and block out the light of this Sun of God, which equates to the goldenness of Absolute Love, like clouds. These Higher Authority figures affect all of us, starting with parents, or other elder family members who are likewise enslaved and conditioned by the barbaric continuum of our predecessors' beliefs. Up next on the chain of command is the teachers, certain stories and books, the bosses at work and the governing bodies of our country that command other enslaved human beings by the power of fear and reprimand to enforce and uphold their control. Above the government, at the top of our Fearful Authority Hierarchy it's the Great Almighty; whoever that is in your particular location and cultural orientation. Most governments employ the Almighty to do their bidding like a bailiff, threatening the people with fear of the Almighty's reprimanding hand, as if their own punishments weren't enough. Over time and repetition this coagulation of authoritative voices begin to sound a lot like our voice, governing our thinking and running amok in our heads like a squabbling pack of wild geese that make no *actual* sense.

The smorgasbord of controlling authorities' voices and beliefs can be overwhelming. We feel helpless, stuck, fearful and incapable. Have we forgotten that we possess an innate power that is Life given?

Yes, I think so.

Why?

Because we surrendered it to them as soon as we were out of nappies; the crime of being our true selves did not fit the punishment, so we adapted. Complied. Then forgot.

Now we fear saying, "Please forgive me" because we fear it is true. We fear and believe that we are in fact wrong. That we are at fault, we did do something bad, even if we don't remember doing it and it denies our own survival instinct to guiltily confess it to an authority which presides over us.

You didn't do anything 'wrong'. You were born human, and to be human is to err; to grow and evolve. Like a child learning to walk we fall down, we get back up, we brush ourselves down and have another go. Generation after generation, we get back up have another go, try to stand on our own two feet as self-empowered unique and amazing individuals. We are always the new generation on the brink of the cutting edge of the epoch of the evolution of human consciousness. And as we evolve, like a sculpture, wouldn't it stand to reason that our maker also grows, learns, and evolves like the Sculptor? Consciousness is a living, breathing entity seeking to know itself infinitely. Perhaps we are the result of a love affair between maker and making, writer and song, painter and painting, sculptor and sculpture.

What About Sin?

What if the true definition of sin was grossly misinterpreted all those years ago? What if it is true that we sin from the moment we are born and will do until death, and perhaps even lose our mortal soul? Could 'sin' be a description of harboured fears and doubts that no-one has yet told us is okay, normal and human to have, and that EVERYONE feels?

Instead of 'bad' deeds, could sins be related to *hidden thoughts and feelings* that when left mouldering within us, unseen, unheard, and misunderstood, creep in like haunting shadows, slowly spreading like the Black Death, destroying our humanity and even the very fabric of our worldly existence?

We all inherit baggage. What is within us, and part of us will inevitably come out of the woodwork and be seen on the surface. The big picture is that within each mortal man and woman there is darkness, shadows and rotten masses; burial mounds of fear and 'bad' feelings. Each individual's suppression eventually manifests a plague of dis-ease, capable of spreading throughout the world. A world which we conveniently prefer to distinguish as 'separate' from us, not our responsibility and way out of our control.

On this larger scale you could say that we are all victims. We are all slaves to either physical pain, mental strife, emotional damage and spiritual havoc. Very few people know where to turn and what to believe in any more. Most cling to what they've been taught, and some dare to venture out and find a more loving, more digestible and acceptable alternative. Some just give up and die because the problems are too overwhelming and unbearable. They need immediate relief; a way out.

We can readdress the harmony. We can heal the wounds we inherited. We can stop passing them on to the next generation. We can begin to reverse the trends and clean up what we have been victim to all our lives. We can reclaim our power.

But it will mean owning our mess and to stop blaming '*them.*' It means asking for forgiveness.

When Forgiving Means Letting Them Off the Hook

Who do you have resistance to forgiving, maybe a relative who betrayed you, a lover who wronged you, a teacher who beat you? It could be someone you don't know personally, but have read about in the news, the atrocities of warring governments or murderers and rapists that sicken you.

Why Should You Forgive Them?

Because **You** need it.

Because all the time (and you have so little of it) that you spend caught in a drama, embroiled in a story, even a really good and righteous tale of good and evil, as we learned a few chapters ago, it's not the Ultimate Truth. It just **appears** that way to us, from our perspective. You've got yourself sucked right in to the middle of the oldest tale in the book about good versus evil. Fighting with it, ignoring it, suppressing it and hating it obviously hasn't helped or it would have worked for us by now.

Don't we have to use a different medicine when the one we've been using to fight disease with for the past several thousand years has not given us the cure? Let's change tactics. Free yourself for your own sake. Then pass the knife to the next man and show him how to cut his bonds free. Some men would rather stick their neck out, toughen up and die proud and fighting than to cut their own ropes and admit that they'd rather snuggle up in a warm blanket of unconditional love instead. But yawn.... boring. Been there, done that - NEXT!

What Have *They* Got To Do With You?

Everything. This is your home too. You live on this planet, you inherited the Earth along with all the people: the pollution, the pain and the history. What happens here is your business. Don't just make money out of it and reap a living from it. Invest your energy and attention within your sphere of influence. Clean your own back yard. Make a difference to where your powers can reach, starting with where you are right now. I dare you...

"Forgiveness is not always easy. At times, it feels more painful than wounds we suffered, to forgive the one that inflicted it.
And yet there is no peace without forgiveness."
—Marianne Williamson

How To Forgive Other People

Wouldn't we rather hear someone else saying it to us because then they've admitted their guilt and taken responsibility for our pain?

Justified though we may feel, that wouldn't feel quite right either. We are still giving them our power, remember?

But what if it really is someone else's fault that you've experienced pain and suffering? Why should you forgive THEM? Surely they're the bad guy, shouldn't they be the one asking for forgiveness?

So many times I've heard my clients, friends or family members say they have forgiven the people who've hurt them. When I asked how they did it, they say, "Well, I said, 'I forgive you'" and they mostly did it in their mind, silently. Sometimes it was out loud, they spoke the words 'I forgive you' and pictured the bad guy in their mind, or looked at a photo. They can swear they did their forgiveness work, and yet they STILL FEEL bad, ill and unhappy.

So what's missing? How can we be thorough and sure that we've changed our story and even changed history for good; forever?

Let me show you this.

The Art Of Forgiveness

Whoever you have pain associated with, your bad guy, draw them here:

A rough sketch will do, but go for it, however you want to do it.

This is how I do it....

'Bad Guy' person

Now draw You, near to them in the picture.

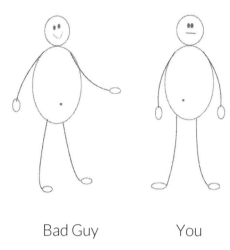

Bad Guy   You

Where does it hurt in your body or mind in this scenario? Make a big dot on the picture of you to show where your pain is located.

Now make a mark on the person where you want them to feel your pain.

Draw a line between the two marks. If there are many painful places mark them as dots and draw all the matching lines between the two points: From you to them, or to them to you. Wherever you feel they should be. Make the connection.

Like this:

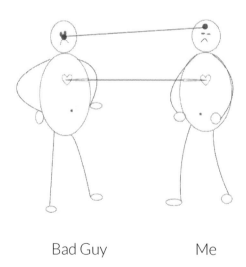

Bad Guy   Me

Can you see how attached you are to the person you're in conflict with? These lines represent your mental, emotional and spiritual bonds with each other. The person you've drawn may also have a few of their own lines connecting to you that you are not aware of.

The places where you've made dots of pain are called the 'trigger points' or pain-body 'buttons'. This is why we say that someone is "pushing my buttons!" They are YOUR buttons that have been pushed and activated. You can argue that the other person created your pain button and it wasn't there before they did something to you and that **they alone** are responsible for your pain, but because of what I know about your birth blue-print, I'm going to state the fact that the button was there in your blue-print beforehand; awaiting a **specific catalyst** (the person/people who you blame for your pain) to trip the switch and set off **your pain alarm.** These bonds are a spiritual soul contract, to enact these issues between you for the purpose of evolving your consciousness.

Look how the lines between you indicate where you have a deal set up, where you both get to feel something because you triggered each other's pain body buttons. See if you can step out of reaction for just a moment.

Take a breath.

Observe that you are both chained together by your pain, despite whose fault it appears to be that you became this way. If you want to change the deal and get out of this messy, emotional reaction bondage, you need to do what is necessary to remove the chains. Do you agree?

Cutting and running from the other person or situation has long-term repercussions. Your pain-button will still be tender and vulnerable to re-attachment from another person. It's your button remember, so even if you cut the cord, the button needs to be de-activated so that you can heal. Have you noticed that when you leave one intimate partner relationship you seem to get a similar pattern repeating in the next relationship? Or if you have a boss that aggravates or bullies you, thus you quit your job and get another, only to run into a similar story in your next job? Do you ever wonder WHY people consistently attack you, bully you, abuse you, use you, complain about you, or something else repetitively unpleasant? It's because you are open to it. Not consciously in your mind, but subconsciously, and in your emotional pain body you have the tendency; a primed pain button; awaiting activation by anyone with a similar or opposite pain button wound to you.

Think of it like a mini magnet that will magnetise towards itself the exact same magnitude of issue but in opposite form, like a + and - of a magnet, or an infrared signal broadcasting a frequency that subliminally attracts the same frequency of signal in someone else. I call this 'Vibrational Matching'. It's a basic universal law of like attracts like, and opposite attract; both are true.

"Forces always come in pairs — equal and opposite action-reaction force pairs."
—From Newton's third law

The Equal And Opposite Of Everything Is True

That's why it's paradoxical and difficult to understand why an innocent victim would attract a mass murderer. The universe consistently seeks harmony through balance. If someone is very, very strong in their victim signal, they will attract a similarly strong attacker signal. The opposite ends of the spectrum need something of the other to become balanced.

Or the victim will also attract a similarly helpless victim as their equal to pair with, and both will have to battle it out in the victim stakes to see who is the bigger victim. "My dad is poorer that your Dad!" "My bum is fatter than your bum!" "My scar is bigger than your scar!" etc. These two victims might end up having a fight and wind up attacking one another in fear of losing their 'I'm the biggest Victim' status, justifying that it's the other who is the real bully.

The likelihood of the attacker also having been, or still being, a victim of abuse and suffering is about 100%. Like attracts like.

We get really dramatic and emotional about it because we are human, but it is basically down to physics. It's a disaster waiting to happen, as they say and we tend to go to extremes.

So, back to your drawing...

If you cut the cords from yourself but leave the other ends flailing around like live wires from the other person, they will inevitably have to find someone else to attach their cords to so that they get their issues met, their pain seen and wounds healed. They will keep repeating behaviour and patterns until the original button has been deactivated and no longer sends an unharmonious and out of balance signal. They can't help it, they must. It's an unconscious instinct that drives them, whilst they may be blissfully unaware of the havoc they are wrecking.

Similarly with you, if the other person has cut their cords from you, cut you off, let it go, buried the hatchet, walked away, **or whatever**, are you left feeling as if you still carry their story and that they dumped on you? Would you still feel wounded and a bit tender if someone were to poke around in your issue a little bit, like a knife in an unhealed bullet wound?

You could also think of it like an umbilical cord between you. You have an attachment that has grown over time and is a conduit for much information. No matter where you cut the cord, then ends still need to be tidied up. The mother must expel the placenta and the baby must have the cord end tied to stop any kind of contamination from the external environment. The whole thing has to be disposed of responsibly, either by incineration, burial or flushed out to sea. Some people practise a deeper honouring of the placenta and umbilical cord, myself included. We believe that the placenta and umbilical cord served a spiritual purpose necessary to growth and bonding, as well as physically between the mother and child, and not therefore just a bit of unwanted waste to mindlessly get rid of. Perhaps this kind of bond is deserving of a more ceremonious release, as we would afford to a departed loved one who's flesh could no longer serve life?

This is really important. Seriously, Do This Now. Please go to Step 4 Exercise 2 in your workbook and find out who you're attached to that's keeping you in pain

~ Thank you.

It is with this kind of reverence that I would encourage you to consider cultivating towards the bond that's been made between yourself and another, whether it's with your mother or your enemy. The cord exists for your mutual growth; for your mutual transformation. You'll become a more evolved, loving, humble and wise person for practising this art of forgiveness, so why not make it ceremonial? All you need to do it be present, focused and ready to see a whole new perspective.

Denial and non-willingness to heal issues between us, where both parties cannot agree to take appropriate responsibility and make proper amends has been going on for a long time! You could say we have somewhat of a backlog.

These umbilical-like bonds do not simply rot away when our bodies do. They are recorded in the soul's library. The unresolved court file of your individual case will be re-served and re-appear in your next incarnation, as well as continuing to echo through your soul and psyche for the remainder of this one! It's well worth the small amount of effort it would take to resolve this part now rather than adding it to the pile. Clean up as you go along. And do it beautifully.

Don't put off until tomorrow what you can do today."
—Benjamin Franklin

7 Directions Of Forgiveness

Forgiveness is a two way street. And, it has 7 directions, like the directions of your life. To do the most thorough job, we need to clean all 7 directions of pain and cords of attachment, which looks something like this....

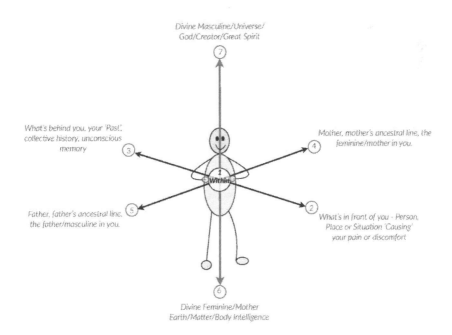

Divine Masculine/Universe/
God/Creator/Great Spirit

What's behind you, your 'Past', collective history, unconscious memory

Mother, mother's ancestral line, the feminine/mother in you.

Father, father's ancestral line, the father/masculine in you.

What's in front of you - Person, Place or Situation 'Causing' your pain or discomfort

Divine Feminine/Mother Earth/Matter/Body Intelligence

Do This Now

Direction 1 ~ Within

Bring your hands to your heart.

Always start at Home, with You.

You are closest to you than to any other being or situation, and whatever bothers you is **your business.**

Where is your pain located in your body or mind?

Remember Step 1? Breathe & Feel. Connect. Put your hands there. *"Hello Me"*

Step 2 ~ Decide to transform. Breathe into it by allowing the spirit of your breath unconditional access to the centre of the pain.

Step 3 ~ Say out loud *"I'm sorry me, that you are in pain because, _____ (describe it, name it) right here."* Keep allowing the breath to flow unhindered.

Step 4 ~ Say *"Please forgive me, me, that you are in pain because _____ (name of person) did _____ to you (description) and made you feel _____."*

Which means, you are now choosing to release and give back what no longer serves you, for your highest good. Continue to breathe and feel and allow Life to work its gift with you.

Good! Well done!

Direction 2 ~ What's In Front Of You?

Point your arms out in front of you.

Who is the person, people, or situation that's in front of you, blocking your path to happiness and preventing you from moving forward with your life right now?

Repeat what we just did.

1. Breathe, receive, feel, connect. Put your hands to the place or places on your body where you feel the discomfort whilst you think of what's blocking you.

2. Decide to clear it because you love yourself enough to do so, so that you are free from this problem.

3. This is the part where you rant or confess to yourself out loud how you feel and what your problem is - The Big WHY you are in pain and what your issue is. Do not try to distort or sweeten your truth. Say it like it is. No-one but you can hear you right now (unless of course you're reading this in a public place, in which case put a scarf over your head and say it under your breath, or wait until you're alone!)

Say: *"I'm sorry* _____ *(name the person, people, authority or situation) that I am feeling* _____ *(angry, upset, disappointed, scared, hateful etc) towards you because I think it's your fault that* _____ *(name your pain or block or problem etc)."*

4. Now release. Say: *"Please forgive me* _____ *(name it/them) that I* _____ *you and blame you for* _____ *and* _____ *and* _____ *and* _____ *and it's not fair. Please forgive me that I gave you my power and felt like a total victim to you because I* _____*."*

Go for it. Get it off your chest. Say whatever you have to say to break the chains. You might have to use a lot of energy and gather force within yourself, and express it with some power. You can even say, "Please forgive me that *I don't even want to forgive you,*

I hate your guts and I wish you would die because of what you did to me/my mum/my baby (etc). Please forgive me that I'm so angry and hurt and I don't want to let you off. Please forgive me that I want you to be in as much or more pain than I am. Please forgive me that I can't forgive you!" Grrrrrrr!

Now BREATHE. Mouth open, throat soft, surrendered. Let the energy move as the chains break and release all that which has been tied up inside you. Let your Divine spirit of life wash you inside. Relax. Real-Ease.

Thank you!

Well done.

You did great.

Can you feel the hold on you lessening?

Direction 3 ~ It's Behind You.

Hold your arms out behind you, or turn around 180 degrees.

What happened in the past, your past, to bring you to this situation now? You might not even know, or remember, but definitely something happened to set this situation up for you, like a spider's web awaiting your inevitable stumble.

Maybe it's your pattern? Maybe it's part of your soul's destined journey to have this experience? Whatever is it, forgive it and release it so you don't have to repeat it, like history always does.

Step 1 ~ Breathe, feel, connect and put your hands where you feel the past attached to you in this situation, even if you have to imagine or guess. Breathe awareness into your back and spine. What might have got stuck there that you thought you'd put behind you? (The past gets stuck in our spine)

Step 2 ~ Is it in your highest good to release it? Are you willing to go that bit further, to reclaim your power that's been held hostage to the past? Decide.

Breathe and receive the feeling of this decision.

Step 3 ~ Say, *'I am sorry everything in the past, that I can see and name as_____ (name it, your history, your pattern) and I'm sorry everything of the past in me that I cannot see or remember which has enslaved me in this disempowering way."*

Step 4 ~ Say *"Please forgive me _____ (name the pattern or ghost of the past) Right now, because I no longer need you"*

Thank you! Well done! I love you! Breathe it through.

How does *that* feel?!

You might need to shake your arms and wriggle your back and bottom now to let the energy from your body move…

Next one…

Direction 4 ~ Left Of You

Birth Mother, Earth Mother, The Feminine

Hold out your left arm at a 90-degree angle and to the left side of your body.

As I've outlined before, Mum has always got something to do with your situation. She made you. Her blueprint became your blue print. You share many cords between you.

I guarantee that whatever your issue, your mother has the same, or equal and opposite of. She holds one end of the problem whilst you hold the other.

Let's cut her free too.

1. Breathe, receive, feel, connect. Sense. Where are you and your mother connected in this blockage of yours? Feel into your body. Put your hands there and hold yourself like a child. What's the connection between her pain and your current painful situation?

2. Decide if your little child is worth freeing. Ask him or her.... *'Hello little me... is it in your highest good that I forgive Mum because you are worth setting free from this cord of pain?"* If the answer is "Yes" proceed to step If "no" please forgive yourself and your mother for thinking you are not worth saving. Thank you.

3. Say, *"I'm sorry me that you're tied to your Mum in this situation. (Save yourself first) And I'm sorry Mum that I'm carrying your pain and acting it out on your behalf........."* (continue speaking it all out)

4. *"Please forgive me Mum that I'm having to work this out in my own life now, and in a way, I'm doing it for you because you were not able to resolve this issue in your life. The burden has fallen to me. Please forgive me that I am fed up carrying your burden and being responsible for what you could not heal. Please forgive me that I feel.......... (name the emotions and feelings) being responsible for something that you were not able to resolve completely."*

Continue to name out everything that you feel to be entangled in with your Mum, around the situation that we started with. You will start to see many more angles appearing as your perspective opens and your awareness increases. Continue to breath and feel compassion for yourself, for your little you, and for your mother. Melt all chains with a "Please forgive me" as you speak the pain out loud. You know when you've done it right because you'll gain a sense of expansion, lightness and your heart will open. Your eyes will feel clearer.

Continue to name out everything that you feel to be entangled in with your Mum, around the situation that we started with. You will start to see many more angles appearing as your perspective opens and your awareness increases. Continue to breath and feel compassion for yourself, for your little you, and for your mother. Melt all chains with a "Please forgive me," as you speak the pain out loud. You know when you've done it right because you'll gain a sense of expansion, lightness and your heart will open. Your eyes will feel clearer.

Breathe.

Thank you for doing that. Your inner child might be feeling a bit wobbly right now, but also quite empowered I should think. Rub your heart and your belly.

Breathe IN. Receive the energy available to you now, soft, open and yielded like a blossoming rose. And allow the breath to carry out, with no strain, effort or pushing on your part, all that remains of those stale old feelings. Be gentle with your throat. If it feels tight or blocked, you have not yet fully released the truth that has become stuck in there. There are more words to clear...

Direction 4 is more than just your birth mother, it's the direction of the feminine within you, the soft, gentle, fierce, feminine, motherly power. Your energy here is the indication of your relationship with the Divine Feminine, Earth Mother, Mother Nature. It represents your connection with your birth and embodiment upon earth. Any issues you have about being HERE, in this body, on this earth; everything you think, feel and believe which limits your expression or joy, which wounded you as a child, need to be forgiven from this direction. It's like cutting the umbilical, along with all the cords of conditions and attachments that have kept you stuck in a limited, small or child-like version of yourself in your life, and finally being able to stand freely on your own two feet.

When we have strength of consciousness to go to the most tender and vulnerable places within us, to meet the tiniest little 'me,' we are doing such great and illuminating work. Lighting a match of awareness in the scariest, loneliest darkness takes courage. When we are tired of fearing and not knowing, it takes true heart to choose to see. To no longer blindly fearing but notice what's hiding there waiting to be found in the shadow lands of our soul and psyche. And it is still brave to descend into the depths with a friend, a partner, a healer, or soul midwife. You do not have to do this alone. In fact, it's better shared. The conscious witnessing of one person is heroic. The conscious witnessing of two or more is the route to epic reality shifts.

Well done. Thank you for getting this far. I love you.

Direction 5 ~ Right Of You

Father, Father Spirit, The Masculine

Hold out your right arm at a 90 degree angle to the right side of your body.

Do the same as before, only now we'll see the flip side, or mirror, of what we just did with your mum. Imagine a strip of velcro, the fabric hook and loop fastener that's made of two equal but opposite pieces that perfectly stick together. Let's imagine one side is your mum. The other side is your dad. Two people with physical, mental, emotional and spiritual hooks and loops that became attracted to each other and fitted each others' stories perfectly. Thus they became joined and you were created; the innocent and magical union of all these hooks and loops. You will feel the memories recorded within you somewhere, of every hook and loop belonging to your parents. Loops are a metaphorical term for the passive aspects to their story, i.e., victim consciousness, innocence, ignorance or lack of something, like confidence, power or money. Hooks are the metaphorical active aspects, for instance; the bully or aggressor, the go-getter, powerful, dynamic, deliberate or conscious aspects. Both passive and active are alive within the relationship and participating equally. Therefore, both aspects are active within you.

We can think of the loops as feminine or passive energy and the hooks as masculine or active energy. Role reversal in our parents is very common however, so the mother may be dominant and aggressive (even passively) whilst the father is yielded and passive (but aggressively disempowered).

What, in your painful issue, is similar to your father? What could you have adopted from his psyche as your own without realising?

1. Breathe, receive, feel, connect and sense. Where are you and your father connected in this blockage of yours? Feel into your body. Put your hands there and hold yourself like a child. What's the connection between his pain and your current painful situation?

2. Decide if your little child is worth freeing. Ask him or her.... *'Hello little me... is it in your highest good that I forgive Dad because you are worth setting free from this conditional pain?"* If the answer is "Yes" proceed to step 3. If "no" please forgive yourself and your father for thinking you are not worth saving. Thank you.

3. Say, *'I'm sorry me that you're tied to your Dad in this situation. (Save yourself first) And I'm sorry Dad that I'm carrying your pain and acting it out on your behalf........* (continue speaking it all out)

4. *"Please forgive me Dad that I'm having to work this out in my own life now, and in a way, I'm doing it for you because you were not able to resolve this issue in your life. The burden has fallen to me. Please forgive me that I am fed up carrying your burden and being responsible for what you could not heal. Please forgive me that I feel .... (sad, angry, lost etc) being responsible for something that you were not able to resolve completely."*

Continue to name out everything that you feel to be entangled in with your father around the situation that we started with. You will start to see many more angles

143

appearing as your perspective opens and your awareness increases. Continue to breath and feel compassion for yourself, for your little you, and for your Dad. Melt all chains with a 'Please forgive me' as you speak the pain out loud. You know when you've done it right because you'll gain a sense of expansion, lightness and your heart will open. Your eyes will feel clearer.

Thank you for doing that. Well done. I love you.

Direction 6 ~ The Below

The Earth, Birth, The Ancestors

Let your arms drop to your sides, completely relaxed, surrendering to what is earthtly.

Look at your feet standing on the ground. Beneath you are countless layers of history, buried stories of the people who walked the earth before you; your personal family ancestors, all our inter-relations, interconnections and interpretations of life. Here you are, adding your layer to the story. If life is a stage for a play to play out, and the story has become boring, tedious, repetitive or debilitatingly un-extraordinary, then perhaps we can change the scene? Time for a set change! You are the new set my love. Set your scene, set your story straight. What can you acknowledge of the past and of your ancestors that graces and honours them, whilst also bringing awareness to what no longer serves you, or your children and all future generations of this planet?

Step 1 ~ Breathe, connect, feel. Sense it in your bones, your blood, your roots below the surface. Allow your consciousness to slide right down into the base chakra area (your bottom, perineum and sexual organs) of your body and beyond. Say, *"Hello ancestors of Me."*

Step 2 ~ What are you done carrying the baton for, and now choose to put down?

Step 3 ~ *"I'm sorry to all of you who carry this same or similar pain that I do now. I'm sorry that you didn't have the support, love and consciousness to heal it the way I have now. I'm sorry that you all suffered and were stuck in the historic pattern of your ancestors too. I'm sorry that I have been stuck with your issues and until now have not been able to resolve it, for you or for myself. I'm sorry that I'm having a problem with what I have inherited from you."*

Step 4 ~ *"Please forgive me ancestors, for all your suffering and pain. Please forgive me that you took it to your grave. Please forgive me that this part of you never came to light for love and healing. Please forgive me that I didn't realise that I could clear it from all of us until now, and please forgive me that I have blamed you because I inherited your patterns and suffering. Please forgive all of us, Mother Earth, that we hold onto our pain and suffering and remain unconscious to the truth. Please forgive us that we forget that we are your children and that we can give all our pain back to you, that you can release and heal us with your unconditional divine mother love."*

Let your unconditional breath of Creation relieve you now of your pain. Let it wash through the places where you have carried the pain.

Thank you.

Direction 7 ~ The Above

Heaven, God, Great Spirit, The Universe, Deities & Religious Icons

Raise your arms above your head, reaching for the sky, finally, giving it all UP; surrendering to the Divine. Our spirits are all in unison, experiencing this journey of being human collectively. Within our individual psyche, and within the collective, we are all imprinted from traditions and religions of judgemental and unkind Gods and authorities who presides over us and punish us for not being good enough or God enough. We hear these voices of unfair judgements and condemnations in our heads daily, even if we don't necessarily subscribe to particular religious beliefs consciously.

It's one of those things that gets heftily scarred into our heads without proper resolution for generation after generation. We have to ask ourselves if this kind of judgment is actually good for us, and works to keep us happy, healthy and sane? Do these beliefs serve you?

If not, are we willing to give them up and set ourselves free? Perhaps there's another experience of the Divine waiting to be felt which seeks no appeasing, has no interest in admonishment, grants neither approval nor permission and refrains from judgement altogether?

Step 1 ~ Breathe, connect and notice that the breath has no harsh tones or judgement, for it has no mind. We are the ones who can think about the breath and then try to block it, disallow it, control or manipulate it. The breath just IS. Place your hands on the top of your head and feel the place where judgement comes from. You may even sense the energy above your head. Imagine a column of light streaming from above you and entering through the top of your head. What is the source of this light? Notice the qualities of it. Is there anything blocking it or altering its purity? *"Hello God-Me/ Divine-Me/ Light of Me"* (choose your own words)

You may feel an oppressive weight or heaviness, or you may feel pulled out of alignment with it. What comes between you and the unconditional source of light?

Step 2 ~ Let us choose to ask the source of light to lift it from us, and for ourselves to release anything which seeks to control, manipulate or darken our spirit.

Step 3 ~ Say *"I am sorry, me, that you are tapped in energies of power and judgement, control and manipulation that feel bigger than you and beyond your reach. I'm sorry me that you're a victim of collective consciousness and are being caught in the rip tide of beliefs and programming that are not truly yours."*

"I'm sorry Breath and spiritual energy of me that I don't fully trust you and try to control how I receive you. I'm sorry that I have fear of being controlled or let down and that I feel scared to trust life."

Step 4 ~ *"Please forgive me higher authorities of me that I no longer agree to you taking precedence over my mind and dominating my beliefs. Please forgive me if I'm unconsciously giving you power and please forgive me if you think you're allowed to have power over me."*

"Please forgive me Breath and spirit of me that I block you, resist you and fear you. Please forgive me that I am not fully receiving you and opening up to the greater presence that I Am."

Thank you. Thank you. Thank you.

Breathe and feel everything as the words wash through you.

My words are a guide and may not be exactly right for you. If you have your own words spontaneously springing up to be spoken as if finally their chance has come, then please allow them. I encourage you to find your own voice with this. Make it real. Make it authentic. Make it your own conversation.

I love you. Well done.

And bless you for having a go and trusting me to guide you this far. In a way, this is the hardest bit. We're in the peak of the journey. It's been a bit of push to get to this summit of honesty, humility and realisation. It's all downhill from here on in. We are now cruising homeward bound.

Pat yourself on the back.

The Quick Version

So, that was quite a lot to take in. But now you know the 7 directions you can have the quick version. If it's a big issue you're dealing with I heartily recommend spending the time to cover all directions thoroughly. With practice and **as you develop your awareness** your inner landscape will become more familiar to you, and like accessing files from your office cabinet you'll quickly pull up the information from your psyche that you need to reference.

Developing your awareness is an important part in all of this. It's bit like, if you want to ask a favour of someone, the least you could do is look at them whilst you're asking and see who it is you're talking to. It's vital to have some sort of connection with the direction our pain comes from because this connection is the passageway which allows the energy between you, physical and non-physical, to move. (Remember the umbilical cord)

Therefore, pay attention to the direction of the attachment. Get it clear in your mind, or feel it as powerfully as you can. Become aware of the unknown that you don't yet know, just by focusing your attention on the area that is dark or blind. Get a sense of the cords that are coming out from you, like in the 7 directions of forgiveness diagram. Get a sense of all the space around you, and take it in. Breathe. Become Aware. Remember that you are asking for all chains, bonds, contracts and attachments that are not serving your happiness and growth to release from you, for good, **forever.**

Once you have become familiar with what each direction is, we can simply say any of these statements that feel best to you, substituting words like God or Gaia for whatever feels right to you. You might like to say all three.

"Please forgive me future, past, Mother, Father, God and Mother Earth of me."

"Please forgive me all directions of me."

"Please forgive me all dimensions and timelines of me; all aspects THAT I AM."

Thank you.

Notice what you feel. Is the space around you now feeling light and clear?

Some things are stubborn to let go of so easily and require 1:1 attention. When you value your freedom, you will attend to these places diligently. However, we aren't finished yet. We're only mid-way through the process, with 3 other vital steps that need to take place before you feel fully liberated and happy again.

This is probably the most difficult step to take because of all the concepts, ifs, buts and maybes we have about forgiveness. If it were that easy I expect more people would have done it by now. It truly does take the heart of an angel to become so humble. Or the heart of a lion to be so strong. Or the heart of a child to be so innocent and forgiving. Or the heart of a very unhappy man or woman who finally, despite all the odds, eventually, if reluctantly, is willing to face their struggle and cut themselves free from the pain.

Whatever it took for you to do all that work, thank you. I for one appreciate your efforts and understand what it took for you to do all that. Well done. You have made a difference in the grand scheme of things. Sometimes it's a huge effort just thinking about it! That's why you shouldn't dwell on the process too much at all, just jump right in and begin with a deep breath.

> *"To err is human, to forgive divine"*
> —*Alexander Pope*

I love you.

Loving Reminder

-STEP 4-
I LOVE MYSELF ENOUGH TO RELEASE AND LET GO WITH THE MAGIC KEYWORD 'FORGIVE'

- ❖ I love myself enough to forgive and release myself from what I no longer want or need in my life, for good.

- ❖ Asking forgiveness has nothing to do with me being bad or wrong and everything to do with me saving and re-claiming my true self.

- ❖ I can only release what doesn't belong to me or what no longer serves me to hold onto. What's truly mine stays.

- ❖ Forgiving myself and others has nothing to do with hierarchy or false power and control. All beings are equal. I can free everybody.

- ❖ Forgiveness requires my humility. Humility opens me so that I can release what I've held on to.

- ❖ Forgiving myself and all others liberates me, which is empowering!

- ❖ Forgiveness is always a two-way street. I am as attached to what causes my suffering, with contracts I may not realise or remember making, as much as the other is attached to their end of the bargain.

❖ It's not my fault but it is my business to clean up the mess in me.

❖ Forgiveness has 7 directions: Within me, my future or what's in front of me, my past, my feminine/mother, my masculine/father, my earth and ancestors, and my spirit/god/the great above. I forgive myself first, then release others.

❖ I honour this process and myself. What I'm doing is a big deal on many levels, even ones I cannot yet see, or that others will see, or will ever see.

❖ I trust my feelings to guide me when forgiveness is complete or not. The better I feel the closer to my truth I am. The worse I feel, the further from the truth I am.

❖ I feel especially relieved, empowered and free to forgive what I most resist forgiving. I forgive everything until I feel good.

❖ Forgiveness is my nature, as a small child I could forgive anything.

❖ I love myself enough to forgive everything and be free.

True Stories

"I love you, me." Wow four words that have truly changed the way I see, experience and FEEL life.

Prior to meeting Tara, I had been on a quest to rediscover who I truly am; to expand, discover, prove, call it what you may, my inner knowing or greater consciousness. It had been quite a journey to that point, with inner walls coming down, albeit not completely. While I navigated the confusing road of the present Spiritual trends, expanding my awareness and generally becoming a better human being towards others, there was something that always stood in the way of further progression, and I simply could not understand what it was or how to get around it.

I just couldn't seem to figure out why my own life didn't seem to connect, 2 + 2 didn't equal 4. I felt stymied, confused, frustrated, angry that none of what I was hoping to achieve personally, mentally, professionally, or socially was coming to pass.

Along came this rather tall lady from the UK named Tara. I didn't know what to expect at first as I had plenty of other teachers and mentors at that time. Tara asked me what was I there to achieve; "...where am I going?..." and it was the first time I had heard the words "I Love You Me."

In the book "Love Without End" by Glenda Green, Yeshua (Jesus), tells Glenda, "...you cannot love another until you fully love yourself..."

This concept was foreign to me, too narcissistic, why the heck would I stare in a mirror and utter such crap. Well, let me tell you, after that first instance in which Tara had me search for ME, I still wasn't convinced. However after subsequent visits and finally embracing the concept of the "I Love You Me," my life has truly changed in ways that I had hoped and dreamed of.

It was a painful awakening to my inner ME, much like coming across an abandoned family pet shivering in the rain, cowering in fear, wondering why his or her beautiful world has been torn apart. Realising it is alone, then thinking that he or she will never be loved again, when all he or she has to give is nothing but unconditional love. This is whom we are inside, that inner ME whom I abandoned and completely forgot about, threw out in the trash of life, ignored all MY pleas for help, for acknowledgment, to love ME for whom I am and yet completely shut out.

Tara helped me to embrace ME, to love ME, to reconnect with ME, to become one with ME and in doing so brought clarity and meaning to my life with ME again.

Saying, "I Love You, Me," opened up parts of my being that I thought I had cleared with previous Healers, only to discover that wasn't the case. At times it was very painful, confusing, loving, more pain as blocks cleared, greater love as that love of ME emerged and was filled with light.....finally!

One day I sat begging for forgiveness for all I had done to ME and then the flood gates opened. Suddenly I found myself begging for forgiveness for whom I had become, actions I taken against others, things I had said, memories buried deep, hurts, anger and revenge that was tucked away in my Being somewhere to be used against another in the future. I literally screamed for forgiveness to God, my wife, friends and ME. I was crying, trying to breath, or rather gasping at whatever air I could take in, ALL AT THE SAME TIME!!!!!

From that day forward, life took an amazing turn for the better. In rediscovering ME, fully embracing and loving ME I have moved beyond those limitations of the previous years, expanded my awareness and now embrace the challenges of our world head on in every moment of now.

As a whole Being once again, I have now moved on to rediscovering whom I truly am. It is far grander than the Gurus and Teachers tell us it is (many Gurus and Teachers are not *aware of the true nature of our Being themselves), and in time we will all rediscover that point, some in this lifetime, others in the next.*

Tara was there, as one of the Souls you run across in your journey, when you reach a crossroads or impasse of sorts. She provided me with the tools, knowledge, Love, to help me progress beyond that crossroad in my life and progress to far greater things than ever I could have imagined.

None of this could have happened had I not uttered those four magical, utterly beautiful words.

"I LOVE YOU, ME"

—David in Dubai, Pilot"

"The practice of forgiveness is our most important contribution to the healing of the world."
—Marianne Williamson, Author

LOVING MYSELF ENOUGH
TO LOVE EVERY BIT OF ME

Love – The Answer To Everything?

What if love was the answer to everything? We'd probably brush it off as too simple an answer for all the world's magnitude of issues and problems, or we'd run mile because it's too big and mysterious a subject to contemplate. Let's start with the simple and see how we feel by the end of this step. Your feelings are the best guideline for what the greater truth might be.

When someone says to you "I love you" and they REALLY mean it, isn't it the most wonderful thing ever? What is more right on the whole of this planet and in our entire human experience than being truly, unconditionally, no strings attached, out-right loved, for everything that we are? Everyone, good and evil, wants to be loved. Whether we realise it or not, our motivations for all our actions, reactions, purpose and pleasure in life are fuelled by the need for Love.

What would the world look like if every single person felt unequivocally loved?

We base our sense of achievement, success and self-value on how much we are loved and approved of by others. In the face of what feels like rejection or failure, it's the hunger for love that motivates us to rise and try again. We want a significant someone to see us, praise us and give us their blessing of a life well lived or a job well done. It could be Dad, it could be God. It could be an invisible or even imagined source of the ideal love, a standard that we are trying to reach, impress and be recognised by, to give us that 'truly loved' feeling. It's as if there's a goal, a level at which we can finally rest in peace. Perhaps we'll find it in heaven?

Love is surely the greatest mystery because even though we can't see its face, we don't know the meaning of its name, we may not even fully believe it exists, and yet we all know in our core that true love is what we search for, and long to find for our true happiness. It's as if love is everywhere, all around us yet hiding in plain sight, like a fish in the ocean looking for the water.

Unloveable

We are creatures of love. We are designed by and default to Love. Despite being conditioned by the human experience, we all inherently know of a place, somewhere in time and space, where we were loved entirely and without question. The innocent babe within us intuitively remembers the spiritual purity and peace, the feeling of home that was our origin, the place where he longs to get back to. It's why love feels familiar. But on this planet of black and white and paradoxical duality, it seems that true love is nowhere to be found, or else only for the select, blessed few who must hold the secret to the stars in their hands, or something? Or, have been a really good person in their past life to deserve it, (so we imagine). When the horror hits us that this world knows very little about love, and that true love is hard to find, what have we left to trust in? Our world collapses.

The world does indeed seem to be collapsing.

There are those who seem driven to spite love. Somewhere in their soul-story love betrayed them. They felt so unloveable or unloved that they became fuelled by resentment toward love, as if it was to blame for their pain. Their aggressively won victories are a big "Up yours," their actions a bold and painful statement to the world — "I don't need you *or* your love."

Even when the heart has turned dark and love perverted into hatred, underneath the bravado of not-needing stems the same core need to be loved, whether it is recognised and accepted or rejected and denied. They may have closed their heart to feeling the emotions of love, but love is a spiritual energy that permeates all levels of life. We can close the doors to its call and shut our eyes, but it never stops summoning us to its altar. It takes great effort and a mighty will power to resist it, or copious amounts of suppressants to numb us from it. But even Frankenstein needs his bride, Hitler his Eva, Ian Brady his Myra Hindley, and Bonnie her Clyde. Love is not reserved for the 'good'.

A heart can be broken at birth. Whenever the moment hits us as that the Source of Love from which we came is now far away or absent, the only cure is to go searching for a replacement. Can we truly find love in a human world? A huge problem arises if we can't. If we can't find a match, or a return to the love state that we inherently remember, we suffer immensely. We take it personally. We can feel outcast by the Source of Love, kicked out of heaven, expelled from purity and perfection, and dumped unwillingly into this dense quagmire of a situation, here on earth.

Taking It Personally

When we believe (even if it's an unrecognised belief) that we are here to suffer; life is punishment; life is a test; life is a game we have to win or else; to be human is to sin; we are fundamentally unloved, we take everything personally. Every look of a stranger in the street, the comment made by the till operator in the supermarket, the baby that cries when you pick it up, the dog that won't come to you, the guy that beeps you on the road. It's all confirmation that life is against us and we are the victim. Poor Us! Aww....

It must be awful having the whole world against you.

It is awful when you believe that life does not love you enough to give you the love you're looking for. Everything becomes a 'sign' that it's true. The belief that love evades us, thereby making us have to search for it, is another punishment, especially when we don't know what we're looking for.

The Search For What We Don't Yet Know

If true love is a rare find how do we know what 'unconditional love' really looks like? We can search for something with an idea in mind of what it is, or should be, or we want it to be, and compare it to the intuitive memory of the universal or mother love from whence we came. And we can also think about what hasn't matched up to our expectations in the past and compare an idea of love to what we don't want and have rejected. But in solid, down to earth terms, as we descend from the spiritual heights to the day to day needs, have we really any clue what we're looking for?

On this material plane, would we recognise true love when we saw it?

I see millions of people searching for something that matches their ideal of love. We have checklists for love, pros and cons for love, search engines for love and 'find your ideal partner' websites for love. And much to our dismay, love doesn't adhere to our lists. It is as it IS.

Could we forgive ourselves for having had no or very few references for unconditional love when our entire childhoods, like it or not, were riddled with love as a reward, strictly given to us under certain conditions? Love if we look nice. Love if we behave. Love if we don't swear and get good grades. Love when we are nice. Love when Mum and Dad are happy, or no one getting any love when someone is angry. A million little ways that we have been brought up and taught the rules that make love conditional. Even our relationship with the Divine has become conditional. God will send you to heaven if you're good. Santa Claus will give you presents if you're good. Fairy God Mother will come to you if you're good; otherwise, you're all going to hell with no presents and you won't go to the ball!

Love As A Reward

The majority of us were raised under these conditions of 'Being good'; do as we're told, don't complain, to be nice, play fair, **and then** we will be rewarded. Perhaps this worked for us as children. Maybe we learned to suffer in silence nicely to get our treat, approval, or love. Maybe we learned to be very, very good children and help everybody without asking anything in return, as all good children dutifully should. Maybe we took beatings to be loved. Maybe our being good was used to cover and hide the mess of so-called-love that the adults were making around us. Quite possibly we quietly took the brunt of a lot of things that weren't our responsibility and tried to make it better by being good.

Are we naively re-enacting our school years now as adults? Are we still doing our best behaviour, waiting for the treat, approval or love that we so desperately crave, wondering "Have I been good **enough** yet?" Whilst feeling bitter disappointment, resentment, anger and betrayal because the promise has not arrived? Do we pray to God in the same way that we wrote letters to Santa Claus, promising to appease him with our best behaviour so that we might have our begged for wishes finally granted? It might sound nuts but what if something like this is even a bit true? Think of what you learned as a child and ask yourself if you might still be applying the same rules of school to your adult life and your love-life?

If you weren't the good one and you didn't seek to please like practically everybody else, what specific attitude or behaviour did you cleverly adopt in order to manhole cover your deeper desire and need for love and approval? Where did your aggressive rebellion to being loved get you? Might you still be applying that same behaviour and attitude now as an adult? Let's find out.

> **Go to Step 5 in your workbook and complete Exercise 1 now to discover your rules for love and if they are working for you**
>
> **~ Thank you!**

Conditional Love & Better Judgement

Imagine you were conditioned through repetition and over time that new born babies are evil? Or that butterflies are out to kill you? Or that kissing makes you ugly? Or that hugging your mother means you're weak?

It goes against every fibre in your being that **knows otherwise**. Everyone knows that being kissed by our beloved is one of the most beautiful feelings a human being can have, and that newborn babies are pure as the morning dew. We know it's true because **we feel it.** These kinds of feelings are often so powerful that they override any mental or rational process of thinking...Like, 'This kiss is enjoyable because it stimulates the nerve endings in my lips that trigger endorphins to run through my body'. Or vice versa, 'This kiss is yucky because I have someone else's saliva and hormonal excretions touching my mouth.' Being kissed by our true love makes us feel blissful and beautiful, so how could it ever be wrong?

Some things feel so 'right,' and yet we are capable of convincing ourselves otherwise. What makes our heart sing one minute can make our heart ache the next. Most often it's because our 'better judgment' gets in there and surreptitiously twists the knife, instilling doubt. Can things really feel this good, this simple and this easy? Can this 'right' feeling really be true?

Some part of us may always stay vigilant and never totally let go to the flow, especially when it comes to relationship love and the exchange of bliss between another and ourselves. The vigilant doubting 'better judgment' part will look for signs that your feelings of 'rightness' are flawed and not so secure. The mind can be like a worm like that, undermining even the most stable love and 'right' feeling. With the best rationality in the world, it cannot understand love. The mind does not, and will never, fathom the language of the heart and feelings, and so we are vulnerable to our own protective thinking as it stealthily sabotages us; backed up with justification that it's for our own good and to err on the side of caution is better, often to the detriment of our happiness and feelings. What we once related to as pure, loving and safe is unraveled like a wooly jumper and reduced to a useless pile of painful regrets. Fear came and laid her eggs and ate the woodwork of our faith and stability.

Love Is Not A Mental Concept

Love is so big and wide and infinite in every conceivable direction that it cannot be contained in our mind. Our mental faculties are limited, so to receive the unlimited is impossible. And yet we try. We assert a rational 'need' to narrow it down, to create edges and boundaries.

I'll go as far as Birmingham for you (from London), but not to the south of France. I'll climb the stairs to the third floor for you but not the 10th. I'll open doors for you but won't whisk you round a dance floor and sweep you off your feet. I'll promise you forever, but not actually marry you, or cheat on you later if I do. I'll make you dinner and sleep next to you every night, but I won't let you into my secret thoughts and feelings. We all impose our limitations. We narrow the field, we put up partition walls and picket fences and mark off our 'safe' territory. We lock away parts of ourselves for 'safe' keeping. We play 'safe' love by vaulting away the unsafe parts. Love requires openness, so what we're really saying is 'I'm protecting my vulnerability' — which means, 'I'm afraid of loving and being loved.'

Ego Vs. Love

Life happens; events outside of our control, all observed by a little person in our mind that reacts and responds in fear and defence, trying to protect the world we created in our minds. We've identified ourselves as separate. We have a little chip in our brain that informs every other system and function in our body that we are a separate being, independent of any other life form, including the earth and the stars and each other. This little chip fights to preserve its identity, literally as if it were a life and death situation. Are you like this? Is that what's driving you?

This vital little chip is called the ego. It thinks, therefore it thinks it IS. It thinks IT IS the be all and end all. It thinks it is the Boss, that IT is in charge, that there is no bigger one than it, and therefore it experiences itself as alone, often in a tirade of complexes of inferiority or superiority. Its full time occupation is analysing the data stored in the psyche/soul bank, riffling through the files, searching for that one piece of information - The truth of itself. It pulls the psyche apart in attempts to know itself; to find peace. It wants to know what this permeating force called love, is. But it cannot. It doesn't have the faculties. But still it searches. And all the while it can't find the ultimate, unifying, sense-making truth, it builds up beliefs on either end of the spectrum of inferior and superior, almost like a pendulum swinging to greater and greater polarities that can be justified only to one-self. That's enough to drive you crazy. That'll be the thing that gets you diagnosed with bi-polar disorder.

What the ego doesn't know is, that it's very significant, important identity was created by a thousand other identities before it. It was born of pure creative substance, then impressioned with the lineage of your ancestors during gestation and infancy. So what you think is **You** has been developed and added to over eons, just like your DNA.

Love is the riddle the ego most wants to decipher, yet it's also the enemy. Love tempts us into another world where the ego can't follow. Love threatens our self-identity. We've worked hard at figuring out who we are and have a life-time invested in thinking ourselves up, so it's understandable that after all this effort the ego doesn't want to destroy or lose what it has built. In making up our minds who we think we are, we've inadvertently become set in our ways. Our neurological pathways have hardened like the grooves in the record. These grooves, as well as being a prison of perception that's hard to escape, doubles up as a security blanket. Routine, rigid thinking serves us an impression of stability, giving us half-baked conclusions upon which we lay the rest of our views about who we are and the greater reality.

Our ego-projected views of reality are both fantastic and morose; perfect and despicable. Our ideas and ideals all balloon from the ego's tight grip. Castles in the air about love, romance, and our version of the happily ever after hang like pink, glitter covered elephants in the room of our head, whilst the morbid fantasies of what we can't have, who we'll never be and why we aren't loveable sink like battleships to the bottom of our emotional whiskey barrel.

Is it any wonder we don't feel secure and connected in our relationships, or in our lives, when we've fabricated our foundations of love with man-made constructs? What solid ground have we to stand on, that we can trust will not betray us?

> **Go to Step 5 Exercise 2 now. What are the conditions and judgements that you put on love to keep you 'safe'?**
>
> **~ Thank you!**

Darkness, Evil And Love

Just as the ego can naively evade us from experiencing true love in our life, so too can it be malicious.

The lack of love, and the need for it suppressed, is what causes a darkness in the soul. The deeper a person's spirit is pushed down, or let down, or abandoned alone in the dark, the more the ego, the false self-identity, rises. It arises like a shadowy entity, over casting a person, eclipsing their light but thankfully not extinguishing it. Although it's not possible to extinguish love, for it is the energy of everything, it is possible to obscure it from vision, like a cloud obscures the eternal sunshine, or the way things seem to disappear in a magic show.

It's a trick of light and shadow, smoke and mirrors that create illusions. And the absence of love is only an illusion played by those who know how to cleverly manipulate the truth, or who are skilled at denying it.

Think of the classic musical film from 1939 "The wizard of Oz" starring Judy Garland as Dorothy. Do you remember when our troupe of heroes first enter the Emerald City and go into the wizard's palace? They request to meet the powerful wizard himself, and a huge, terrifying head appears in front of them, smoke plumes billowing and fiery columns blazing. In a booming voice the wizard basically tells them they are not worthy of his help, deliberately ridiculing and intimidating them with his larger than life presence. It's Toto, their little dog companion, who reveals the wizard's true identity by tugging at a curtain which hides a booth. There inside is a small old man turning a mechanism of handles and cogs that generate a projected image of this mighty and fearsome wizard on the wall. It's all nothing but an illusion. The wizard turned out to be not that powerful after all, just a lonely, ashamed and unloved little man pretending to be something he wasn't, caught in the trap of needing significance, swinging from superiority to inferiority.

This story perfectly illustrates what I notice, both in people's energy fields and in the manifest world around us: When dark or evil energies are attached to a person's etheric field, which in turn adversely affects their mind, their emotional state and physical wellbeing, I know that behind the illusion of a powerful and fearful presence that seems real is the hidden truth. I speak directly to these entities, evil spirits or demons, and tell them I love them. The basis of their power is the fear generated in their host, and they feed off it. When their fuel line is cut off and love poured on them instead, it's like discovering the old man behind the curtain. The game is over. The illusion no longer works, the spell is broken. It's just like the fairy stories! True love's kiss breaks the curse, well sort of. There's bit more to it than that, but it's nonetheless straight forward and effective. Cast love at the darkness and it switches the light on. The truth can't remain hidden where there is a command for it to be revealed.

Now let's put this in the context of a so called bad person, Adolf Hitler for example. Most people agree he was evil and he was definitely skilled at evoking fear in order to manipulate people to his will. First he built his image with powerful speeches about defending the Germans from communism, which he claimed was created by the Jews to control them. He used the imaginary threat of their rights being taken away to generate fear in those to whom he spoke, and fear begot righteousness. Righteousness begot aggression, and the right wing movement gained momentum, fuelled by an idea. Hitler became larger than life, posting his image everywhere, as we see many other elite people of power do. It's big words and images, and the use of fear that generates such massive followings. People become like sheep to the slaughter, losing all sense of their wits and truth in herds and collective beliefs, afraid to stand for their truth, maybe because they don't know what it is. However, the reversing of such mass hypnosis is simple.

A deep breath helps us regain sentience. Ignition of the heart brain with an inhale of oxygen will initiate a return to cognisance, and consciousness is moved from radical thinking to real feeling. Real feeling is the essence of humanity, and is the gateway to the ultimate truth that resides within us all. All it takes is one person feeling truth to awaken the truth in another. As fear lights another's fear, so too does love, compassion, and words of truth. And thankfully light has power over darkness. The night must submit to day. Light speeds darkness away. Try bringing a bucket of darkness into a lit room and spill it out. It can't be done. Darkness is only an absence of light, and even a tiny bit lights enough to see by.

So now consider some dark or painful area of your life, some shadowy thoughts that loom in your dreams or haunt your mind. Or some dark feelings that you fear to venture into. Or some dark and powerful illness, like cancer that creeps into a person's body like a ghoul in the night. We are hypnotised by our fear, we feel powerless and helpless to such overwhelming things and inadvertently allow them to run amok and dominate us. The same could be said of fear inducing leaders, bosses at work, or stately power heads. All of it is over inflated images causing us to submit in fear. Darkness or illness grow in ego-power as more and more people succumb to it, entranced.

Let's switch the light on and look at it properly shall we? It's all a lie. You hold the power. You are the one with the trump cards of consciousness and the ability to love. But seeing is believing, so you first have to move into the arena of truth within you.

You first need to dive into the infinite vat of pure love within your heart, and bathe there a while to wash off the dirt that's obscured your eyes. You can't reason your way out of this one, and why would you want to, unless you want to be less powerful than those who currently rule you? (actual people or thoughts in your mind). The only reason you might want to disagree with this would be to stay in fear and helplessness to the darkness.

It takes experience to know something different, because you don't know what you don't know. You have to do it, and then be altered and awakened by the experience. Then you know something new.

"Evil (ignorance) is like a shadow —
it has no real substance of its own, it is simply a lack of light.
You cannot cause a shadow to disappear by trying to fight it, stamp on it, by
rallying against it, or any other form of emotional or physical resistance.
In order to cause a shadow to disappear, you must shine light on it"
— Shakti Gawain, Author

So, now you know what to do with dark energies, 'bad' people and evil spirits. Love them to vanquish them! Release your attachments to being less powerful than them. Switch on your light of absolute love to dispel the darkness.

What are you afraid of loving?

Go to Step 5 Exercise 3 for a list of your old beliefs that you can now transform with love

~ thank you!

Messy And Wild

'Relationship love' is something that if we're lucky, we fall into, (debatably), almost by accident, almost predestined, even in the most unlikely of circumstance.

People in love lose themselves and are completely consumed by the fire of love's desire. It makes us wild with ecstasy and beastly hungry for more, as if we've been starved for a thousand years! Perhaps this is why the world's multitude of religions tried to tame the flames and control the conduct between us humans in the past? Perhaps they've tried to save us from ourselves as we fall prey to love's abandoned games and fall fallible to it's delicious temptations? Perhaps it is indeed safer to direct all that mortal passion towards the Divine, becoming wild about God, instead of directing it towards the unholy flesh? Why? Because love is so powerful!

Love makes us lose all sense of rational thinking, It throws caution to the wind and better judgment gets a run for its money. Love upsets homely tables, makes a match of opposites and makes a mockery of morals and rules.

Our pupils dilate, our heart rate increases, we sweat we can't speak properly, eat or sleep whilst under its spell. We cannot control it. Two people so intoxicated are drawn to unify, to meet in body mind and soul. It's as if one aspect of love sees something of itself reflected in the other and is charged with the purpose of unification. Love is magnetic, attracted to itself to experience itself. Love seeks union. It wants exaltation! Its highest expression being a euphoric state of bliss when those magical moments of oneness occur. It is utopia. But love is big, and wild, and dirty and messy, whether you're in the act of making love, trying to sit still in its presence, or birthing the baby that your love made.

Physical love-making is gooey, sweaty and noisy even in the most discreet of embraces. And meditation on love will raise everything unlike itself to be seen, all the rubbish you believe about yourself, all the dirt of your conditioning and all the mess that you live in inside your mind becomes suddenly more illuminated the moment you give attention to your heart instead of your thoughts. My Mum always said, "Love will bring up everything unlike itself." I think she read it here...

"Love brings up everything unlike itself for the purpose of healing and release."
— *Helen Schucman & William Thetford, Authors of A Course in Miracles*

And added to by the beautiful Marianne Williamson:

"...Fear is detoxed, subconsciously brought to the fore whenever love arrives. Once aroused, it will either trigger us or depart from us, depending on whether it is forgiven or punished."

Love can drive you wild and make you crazy. It can make you lose your mind, forget the world and want to hold onto your perfect moment forever. When we have love, what more do we need? Money no longer matters. We burn through money for love, no price is too high. We'd give everything to be loved, we do anything for love, to live our lives in love and to die for love or feeling loved. No mountain too high to scale, no ocean too wide to sail, and no trench too deep to assail into to be with the one we love.

If love leaves us feeling so free, messy, wild and on fire, could that be a reason why we the civilised world trains us towards a more sophisticated, socially acceptable and less dirty love, telling us it's safer? Could this be why conditions are imposed supposedly to keep us safe, but actually effecting to limit our freedom and to distrust what we feel? Are we more controllable and easily frightened when not in a state of true love?

And are we magnificent, powerful, able to achieve anything when we are? Perhaps we are afraid of what love will do to us and undo in us? Do we fear love's power?

"Love Is A Drug..."

...According to 80's pop band 'Roxy Music'. Some scientists agree.

Professor of psychology Arthur Aron at State University of New York has been researching the impact of love on the brain for three decades.

"Intense feelings of romantic love affect the brain in the same way drugs like cocaine or powerful pain relievers do...The reason people are so attracted to cocaine is that it activates the area of the brain that makes you feel good... The same reward area is activated when people are experiencing the intense desire of romantic love."
— Arthur Aron, Ph.D.

The results of his study, in collaboration with long-term pain researcher Sean Mackay, go some ways to explain why love is so addictive and why we would do virtually anything to get it. In some ways you might consider it 'safer' to take cocaine to get the love-drug hit instead of opening and exposing ourselves to messy, wild love that requires us to be soulfully naked and emotionally vulnerable. But it also suggests that love is the best remedy for pain relief. Take away the person we are in love with and what happens? Unimaginable, excruciating pain, like nothing else on earth. It would take deadly amounts of paracetamol to kill this level of heart ache and mental trauma. It's not surprising then that people resort to other kinds of medication, pharmaceutical and recreational, to numb the pain and re-ignite those crucial chemicals of love again, even if it is artificially stimulated.

"He (Arthur Aron Ph.D.) was talking about the neural systems involved with love and I was talking about the neural systems involved with pain, and we realised there was a lot of overlap."
— Sean Mackey, Chief of the Division of Pain Management and Associate Professor of Anaesthesia at Stanford University Medical Center

Pain and pleasure walk hand in hand, and so it seems that where there is pain there is also love. Immense feelings of anguish in the event of the love we've come to depend upon being taken away from us, or the fear of our love's death, will often accompany the heightened states of joy we experience. And after the source of our love has departed from us, when we're hurt and abandoned, we search for the new love to heal our pain. We repeat the cycle, caught in an addiction, either to loss or to love, like the cycle of day and night.

Love Protection

Is it any wonder then that so many, arguably the more sensible ones, might prefer to view love scientifically, as a mere cocktail of chemicals stimulating an emotional response? Or, maybe you want to think of it as a weakness that we should resist?

"To be loved is a strength. To love is a weakness."
— Zsa Zsa Gabor, Actress

To protect ourselves from such potentially suicide inducing states of highs and lows, we might even convince ourselves that love doesn't exist; that it is nothing more than fantasy; a fairytale for children; just wishful thinking for the naive and stupid. If such non-believers were genuinely happy and fulfilled, more so than a happy person in love, I might be inclined to join them. However, I find this not to be the case. I'm more in agreement with the scientists who observe that:

INTENSE LOVE EQUALS LESS PAIN

*"While social science is making strides to understand the underlying framework upon which love is based,
the end product can still take your breath away."*
—Atuttle - of Serrendip Studio - 05/02/2008

When we are in love, what once seemed impossible fades to a mouse's whisper. When we are in love the whole world takes a different hue, no dream is unachievable, no feat unconquerable. Love gives us a power more sustainable, more healthy, more real than any cocaine hit. Love heals a wound faster than any drug. Personally, love enabled me to give birth twice, painlessly, blissfully, peacefully.

A fearsome thing indeed to any agent or agenda seeking to control mankind.

Absolute Love is The Antidote to Fear & Pain.

So, we know that there is pain without love, but can there be love without pain?

This Is True Love

Love Loves Us

What if love is everywhere? An infinite energy that has no beginning and no end, impermeable and constant, omnipresent like life itself?

We **need** to Love and feel loved. To Love is our nature. All of our disharmony, unhappiness, disease and distress is rooted in an experience of love's absence, as if the very oxygen we need to breathe was missing.

What if Absolute Love is always striving to reach and find you, just as you are to it? What if you're so busy chasing around, searching, checking your lists, doing your love manifestations, prayers, vision boards and Feng Shui rituals for what you think love is, that you missed Love's advances towards you?

What if Love extends itself to you daily, moment by blessed moment? Would you see it? Would you reach back? Would you be willing to drop your concepts and be altered, re-aligned and brought back into the life giving arms of absolute unconditional, always present, always there, reliable, trustable, indefinable, immaculate, just-for-you, Real LOVE?

Love knows no limits in teaching us what love actually is. If we are to know the truth of Love, and what love is, does, and feels like, then we need to be really present to the relationship that **love wants to have with us.** We must listen and follow its guidance, and practice love in our relationship with our self. Love patiently hold a forever-space for this embrace.

Love is the guide in relationships with others. Love is the journey and the destination all in one. I cannot think of another, better reason to live, other than to follow love in all that we do, who we are and who we are around. To be in love, be humbled by and dance with love, and to learn to love more wholly and completely. And, to let love show us the places where we hold discordance with love, and to allow love to melt the barriers and shadows that hold us a prisoner from love. Love wants to realise itself; to know itself; to be received and met.

In the words of Leslie Duncan, singer and song writer (also recorded by Sir Elton John):

"Love is the opening door,
Love is what we came here for.
Love is the key we must turn,
Truth is the flame we must burn"

Is Love The Ultimate Truth?

What's truly True, is true and true no matter what we do. No matter what we think, or force ourselves to believe for our 'safe keeping' or in the name of being 'realistic,' the truth will prevail. It has to, like North on a compass; you can't debate or argue with it.

Love is like North. When we are off course, moving away from love and what's right for us, we feel it. We don't feel 'right'. We lose direction. Every navigational instrument in our make-up is designed around our True North: Love. How does your heart feel about that?

The problem is that we have been conditioned and trained out of trusting our compass, and we've been taught not to follow our joy or rightness, but follow instead our 'better judgment'. Just look where that's got us.

I Love You, Me

Self-love means not replying on others for your love needs, like not waiting for others to feed you when you are hungry. You can eat with your own hands.

Following the instinct to eat is natural. Feeding oneself love is natural, but we were taught helplessness, and came to rely on a 'grown-up other'; God, parents, partners, or even our children to love us, whilst we remained un-self-serving and un-selfish.

We ignore the hunger pangs for love and become needy desperate beggars, worsening our condition, hoping someone will notice how badly we are suffering, or decide to be responsible and admit how badly they are treating us. We can blame them and feel unloved, but what they are really saying is, "Feed yourself love – I can't fulfil you" or "your neediness is cramping me by painfully reminding me of my own unmet needs."

We compete for the love stakes in families and relationships, often using pity. Who can be the most helpless one? Who is the one in the most pain? Who has to stand up and take the role of grown up and rescue/save/take responsibility for the other's pain? Every single kind of illness has taken this unmet need for love into form, either physically, emotionally or mentally. It's how we demonstrate that **we will literally be willing to die** unless we get the love we need, and we produce obvious signs of our suffering to attract the attention we desperately need.

JP Sears, a spiritual comedian from Youtube called this condition "Patheticism," where we use helplessness as a game strategy, to either sucker someone else into feeling sorry for us, or to gain the attention, (and therefore power), in order to manipulate them to our meet our needs. Then we conveniently and righteously call those who didn't meet our needs 'Narcissists' or 'Evil,' blaming them for our helplessness and shaming them as selfish or dark.

It's mostly not conscious. We don't meant to do it, any of us. It comes from the child within us who's needs for unconditional love were never adequately met. Those deep wounds must rise to the surface somehow, sneakily avoiding the conscious adult awareness, in order to be seen and healed.

Patheticism doesn't just happen to individuals, it spreads to families, subcultures of society, religious sects and even whole countries of people, who, instead of choosing to help themselves, remain dependant, suffering, victims. It can become an identity. This may sound harsh, but it's true. And it's only harsh to those who wish to protect and defend their ignorance and naivety. You have a choice. You can wait all your life to gain the love from the one you're waiting for. Most die. Because we can love each other with everything we've got, but we cannot fill another's cup if there's a hole in the bottom of it. That hole must be filled by the cup holder: You. That's the place where your love is needed and nothing else will fit.

Ignorance is a choice. The brain is a muscle that we can exercise and put to use, or not. The heart is a muscle that we can exercise and put to use, or not. Both have contrasting, yet complimentary systems of intelligence that once used can change a person's life forever. However, we get trapped in the rodeo ring of thinking, becoming the victim to our own limited awareness.

If love is the true north direction of our lives, then let us follow where it points. Love is an experience. Let us bathe our heart, mind body and soul in the sublime simplicity of it.

Do This Now

Step 1 ~ Breathe and Receive.

Bring your hands to your heart, receive your touch as you would wish your beloved to receive and feel it.

Receive your own attention returning to you, as you close your outer eyes and see yourself within, listening with the ears of a lover during pillow talk.

Feel the part of you, the 'me' within, that needs and wants to be loved,

and out loud say:

"I love you, Me"

And not "I love you, Me" because damn, there's nobody else to say it to you. I love you me because you choose to own what's rightfully yours. To allow yourself to receive what you need for your own happiness and wellbeing.

"I love you me" because you are capable of unconditional love, you've been doing it instinctively since you are a baby, it sits well with you, looks and feels beautiful. And, because right now, you are the one who most needs to hear it and be reminded of it. If you want someone else to receive your love, then it's wise to practise giving it to yourself first to see how good a job of it you are doing.

Love Never Left You

You were never lacking. Love never left you. Maybe people who had abandoned love in their own lives abandoned you, but not love. It lives in you, breathes through you, it is you. Remember that Love itself is unconditional. It is you who put conditions on it and abandoned yourself because you were unable to recognise it, right there in front of you. You abandoned you because you thought you weren't loved. You went hungry because people fed you crumbs, and even though you watched people using their hands to feed one another, you never thought to use your hands to feed yourself the sweet, un-bitter food of love.

Say it again. "I Love You, Me" but this time don't let the words echo round the halls of your mind, let them ring in the vestibules of your heart. CHOOSE to open and receive them like the Godsend that they are.

Voice and sound are part of the gift of your creation, use it not waste it. If you are someone who doesn't have the sound of your own voice in good working order, *find a way.*

Saying, "I love you, Me" in your mind has in no way the same effect as saying it out loud. The sound of "I love you" resonating through the atoms of your matter is like the bells of heaven ringing throughout your temple. Your ears want to hear it. Don't keep it locked up like a secret, shameful in a mind that knows nothing of the glory of love; but deliver yourself from the evil that the lack of love gestates.

Imagine if your mother only said it in her head? Maybe she did. How does that feel to you, sort of nice, or not nice? Don't philosophise and rationalise and be 'grown-up' about it. How does it feel? Good or not good?

What if your father, husband or wife only ever said, "I love you" in their own mind and the words never reached your ears? What if NO-ONE ever said it out loud to you?

Even if the call from within is strong, and you know inherently that Love resides within you and IS you, it's still as natural as a child that the experience be externalised too. Our bodies are 70-90% water, we know this, and yet we still cannot live without drinking. We need love reminded and validated to us over, and over, and over again, as if to drum it into the mind, as if to console the soul after thousands of lifetimes of disappointment and disapproval, slaughter and betrayal.

We are wired to want to be loved from all around us; for it not to be a lonely solitary experience, but for love to be shared, Only then is it fulfilling its nature — to expand, to be omnipresent and everywhere. There is no place that love does not want to reach, touch and bring to life in her fullest, infinite potential.

How Do We Know This Is True?

I had a block for a long time about this because I didn't want to be the one who had to love myself. It seemed self-defeating. I thought I already did love myself and I couldn't figure out why I wasn't getting the kind of love from my family and partners that I so badly ached for. I was reluctant, even defiant about owning the fact that I was in denial! I released the block by taking the expectation off of others to love me in a way that I saw fit and stopped judging them. After acknowledging that my need to be loved was unmet, I went to meet the needy little one in me who needed love, and I loved her.

It goes like this...

Do This Now

"Hello unloved little me that needs to be loved but doesn't feel loved enough."

"I'm sorry you're unloved, and you don't feel loved, and that your need for love has not been truly seen, heard and understood by anyone."

"Please forgive me, unloved little Me."

BREATHE.

Ahhhhhhhhhh....

"I LOVE YOU unloved little me!"

Then say, "Well done unloved little me for coming THIS FAR"

"I Love you, Me"

And breathe again...

Keep breathing and receiving and releasing til the stale old feelings have left and the light of true unconditional love has filled the space.

This is soul gardening — transforming barren lands into blossoming fruitful Edens, and replacing what was in pain with the ultimate reality and truth of all things: LOVE.

"A man sooner or later discovers that he is the master gardener of his soul, the director of his life."
—James Allen, Author

If you did a little bit of gardening every day, what would this garden of You look like? What conditions could you transform within yourself that you no longer want to continue living in? Could you give yourself the optimum fertile ground for personal growth? Now that's what I call self-love.

Would you be willing? Yes or no?

I love you broken hearted little me.

I love you me that has had all of his or her dreams shattered.

I love you abandoned little me.

I love you failure me.

I love you ugly, useless, pathetic me.

I love you un-loveable me

I love you dependent, needy, disgusting me.

I love you too complicated me.

I love you hard, closed and protective me

I love you wobbly, sad and depressed me.

I love you alone, with no-one else to love you, me.

I love you angry me, guilty me, ashamed me.

I love you unattractive, dirty, used, abused, unworthy me.

I love you insignificant, un-powerful me

I love you me that doesn't matter to anyone.

I love you arrogant, offensive me.

I love you me that shines.

I love you me that listens to others so beautifully.

I love you me that is unique and special, and like no other.

I love you me that always does his/her best.

I love you me that loves others.

I love you singing, dancing, talented, playful, funny, happy, quirky me.

I love you beautiful, handsome, bright eyed, radiant and confident me.

I love you me that wants to love but can't.

I love you me that wants to forgive but can't.

I love you needy me that wants to grow.

I love you me that doesn't know how.

I love you all parts of me.

I love You, Me!

Let's get straight to the point. Love will compromise, but don't compromise on love. Love wants nothing more than to be with itself, entwined in an eternal embrace with its own creation - YOU.

You also want nothing more than to be loved, so wholly, so completely, so as nothing can come between you and it. To be IN the Love, to be One with it, where the barriers melt away and all of your 'knowing,' senses and awareness are enveloped in the splendour of union.

You and love want to be together, so why get in the way?

Why compromise that relationship?

Love Is Joy

To love yourself means to keep your instrument tuned correctly. You are attuned to enjoy joy! What feels joyful to you?

What do you think causes you joy?

When we think thoughts that are out of synch with love, it ruins our tuning. We go off key and sound terrible!! We whine and whinge and cry, which although acceptable, loveable and a valid part of your emotional experience, don't get stuck in it. Do yourself a favour, love yourself some more and choose to reset to joy!

Joy is like the spring sun spreading over the frozen lands of Narnia (The setting of fantasy novels by C.S. Lewis), melting the harsh grip of the ice-queen's loathing and dispelling her loveless rein.

Your joy fills the world with more colour, and ripples a higher vibration out into the aching world around you. Your joy causes tightly clenched buds to open and bloom. You affect change.

Love is ph neutral. Pour liberally to any acidic or toxic environment. Love harmonises. Play its melody in any off-key situation.

Dependent Love & Relationships

When you're in pain, feeling weak, helpless scared or alone, what is it you reach for or wish for? A grown up, right? Someone to come make it better; your 'Rock'. When we haven't got one of these, we turn to whatever we feel comforted or most loved or accepted by. It could be a child, a pet, a favourite teddy bear, your church, a tree or something in nature. We look outside of ourselves to gain that steadfast feeling of reassurance. We crave connection and love so much that we will completely numb ourselves with Facebook, Tinder, Snapchat, phone checking and texting, TV, internet, food, sex, porn, anything to fill the gap and meet that need. We are creatures of habit and before we know that we're completely addicted to looking for external connection, and that's how we lose ourselves. That's when you have to want to love yourself enough, in these challenging moments, to come back to you. Make the choice to re-connect; Choose step 1 and step 2 to begin the dance of love and relationship with your Self, that's not dependent upon another.

We are dependent upon others when we are small and helpless – yes. But there comes a point where we can awaken to our own power and abilities to care for ourselves. Whilst we are dependent upon others we remain helpless, incomplete, needing, wanting, longing, hungry, suffering in fear that the hand that feeds us will someday, sooner or later, go. And then what? And then we're alone. An intolerable feeling for most of us, a gap that we choose to fill with dependency upon something else. Stop it. Just stop.

What are you doing?

You are reluctant to grow up and claim your power. We talked about this in step 2, owning your power, and here, it is of the utmost importance that you now decide to love yourself enough to grow from dependency upon another, stop leaning on them, and become stable, secure and able to stand on your own two feet. Depend on you for love. Depend on you to always be there. Depend on you to show up and listen. Depend on you to pick you up and hold you. Depend on you to forgive and heal the hurts. This way is the only way, for depending upon others will never satiate the gap inside that only your attention, awareness and love will fill. You are the only man/woman for the job. And a consequence of you becoming independent is that your 'rock,' your 'other,' will also have the opportunity to grow and become powerful too.

Dependent love relationships look like two wounded children who in the midst of chaos, grown-up problems and a crazy, scary world, latched onto one another for safety and comfort. They are helpless together. It's them vs the world, remaining just like children, never growing up, together. Or two drowning people who hold onto the other because they can't swim, so they struggle on together.

In 'The Prophet'; Kahlil Gibran speaks of marriage:

"Love one another, but make not a bond of love:
Let it be rather a moving sea between the shores of your souls.
Fill each other's cup but drink not from one cup.
Give one another of your bread but eat not from the same loaf.
Sing and dance together and be joyous, but let each one of you be alone,
Even as the strings of a lute are alone though they quiver with the same music.
Give your hearts but not into each other's keeping.
For only the hand of Life can contain your hearts.
And stand together yet not too near together:

For the pillars of the temple stand apart,
And the oak tree and the cypress grow not in each other's shadow."

Independence To Interdependence

The pillars stand apart to hold the roof of the temple. They could not if they were joined at the hip. Although they are together, there is instability and insecurity in a co-dependent marriage, always a fear that the roof could come crashing down at any moment, always a fear that the world around them is against them, or does not support their union. Always a feeling that something bigger is missing in their lives, and a want for something greater that they can't yet see. Alternatively, together yet apart like the pillars creates a sacred space for the enlightenment of others, that they may revel in the beauty and holding that this temple offers. Together yet apart is a sanctuary of love, and a place for celebration of love. This temple offers prayers for the world to be in love.

The oak and the cypress, both tall and mighty trees need space to be so.

In each other's shadow they would be weak, small and not fulfilling their potential for greatness. Yes, they would be weak together, a consolation, but it does the forest an injustice. Their roots would be weak, their shelter insufficient and their destiny comprised. Neither is contributing their best.

Trees stand strong when their roots have space to grow, going deep into the dark, unknown soil of their ancestry and death. There, they find the nutrients to feed the trunk. We looked at this earlier when we explored the idea of independence. But when a well fed trunk bursts in multi directions, spreading many branches of itself, budding and generating fruits and nuts, seeds and sappy elixirs, it feeds the rest of the forest. It is abundant. To grow stronger still, the trees roots entangle with its neighbours, its branches reach out to touch others. It is both mutually supportive and supported. It is giving and receiving. Their shared canopy is shelter for more life, the ground holds stability for new life. Relationships can be like this.

What of the 'Love Tree' you ask, that's made of two who grew entwined in the other to form one? These two grow mutually, surrendered to being unified as one from the beginning. Their growth takes longer as they spiral together, each holding the weight of the other and twisting to meet their expectations. And inseparable, they will fall ill together and die together. They add a rare beauty to the world and a romantic nuance, yet even these two will need to branch out in opposite directions to fully express and fulfil themselves, and to fully appreciate the beauty of life and of one another.

Practical Love, Where Do You Start?

WHAT CAN YOU DO RIGHT NOW TO LOVE YOURSELF MORE?

Love Your Mind

Your mind is your friend when you treat it right. When you don't it will turn against you and become your worst enemy. It's your thinking that gets you into most trouble. Think about that. Self-deceptions and wrong perceptions lead us to suffering.

"Yeah but, *I thought* I could trust him..."

"Yeah but, *I believed her* when she said..."

"Yeah but, *I thought* it would be different/ that I could change it/ that you would change..."

"Yeah but, *I expected* them to be there..."

What you think does not equal the reality.

When your thoughts start to make you feel low, depleted, or downright depressed you are not mastering the machine correctly. It has begun to run you. Reclaim the right to your mind's state. Take a breath the moment you realise you're starting to feel terrible. Remember that these are beliefs you currently fall back on that are not working well for you. They are not the truth. Truth by its very nature *feels* true, not thinks true. Truth is not logical either. It's the North on your compass remember, it feels RIGHT. Therefore give yourself other feelings such as relief, peace and contentment. Truth is pro-life not anti it, so any destructive thoughts you have about yourself or others that bring your life energy crashing down, maybe even causing you to want to take your life away, are definitely NOT TRUE, just badly programmed machinery.

Understand that it's the mind's nature to be curious, inquisitive, analytical and make conclusions on new information based upon what it has previously stored in its memory banks. If you want to have a happy mind you need to clean out all the junk thinking that doesn't work for you and has let you down.

These 7 steps will do that for you perfectly. Everything you've learned so far is the dissolve button. Use it on each belief that doesn't make you feel good and align you with your north.

And love will heal you and re-set you. Choose to love the old story like it's a cute, small, outmoded version of truth that you were very attached to, like a doll or a teddy bear — ahhhh. Bless it!

Bless yourself for believing it was the absolute truth when it wasn't, and love yourself for now realising there's more to it than you previously thought. You did the best you could at the time. You can forgive yourself for thinking something was true when it wasn't. Everybody does it.

Everybody.

Love the gap that the old story leaves behind. Love everything, tangibly and out loud.

The other stored memories will re-arrange themselves according to this new shift in the library. A bit like upgrading the software in your computer, all the old operating systems will have to go through the update. Feed your mind with new versions of the stories, as you've now come to realise from doing the "I love you, me" method. When you clear the old version, the clouds part and the sun can be seen once more. Clarity arrives.

> **Now please go to Step 5 Exercise 4 in the workbook to love all the bits of you that deserve and need to be loved**
>
> **~ Thank you!**

Now that you have a clearer perspective, feed the computer-head new information and new versions of your memories. For instance, if you only have horrible memories of someone and all the bad things they did to hurt you on your hard drive, clear the hurt and you'll uncover all the other memories. You'll start to remember the good things that you can easily love and feel grateful for. Now you have productive back up; stories that support you instead of break you.

A Care Plan

Your mind doesn't work well when you are over tired, falling by default into the most used track ways of your internal processing — it will go to the thoughts you most often think. These can be well-worn highways of destructive thinking or your frequented highroads that lead you to success.

Critical, judgmental, guilty, hateful or fearful thinking literally generates chemicals in specific organs in your body. Regular resentment for instance is super toxic and acidic and will drip, drip, drip down your throat, through the adrenal glands and into the spleen. Fear will go straight to the kidneys, anger to the liver, hate to the heart, grief to the lungs.

Next time you feel yourself being dragged down — stop. Catch yourself. Say out loud so the voice is out of your inner mental environment of sewerage that would see you drowned in it

"I am so sorry me, that I'm listening to this stuff and believing it to be real, and therefore hurting you unnecessarily. Please forgive me for hurting you. Thank you, I love you. And thank you me for noticing in time, I love you me for loving me enough to guard me from pain. Well done."

Give yourself a hug and come back to the truth by breathing and feeling the relief.

Love Your Emotions

Let's imagine, for example, that you feel angry.

Denying or shutting your feelings off is like turning off the water tap and not drinking. Imagine the Earth without water. Like this you will become dry, hardened and completely unable to relate to yourself or others. Life will cease to flow and grow in your world. Blocking the flow is to build a damn. And damned is how you will feel. Your feelings will build up behind the wall, so your walls will have to become thicker and stronger to hold back the flow. But no wall is impermeable, and so you'll spend most of your days defending your walls, plugging the gaps, rigid in your ideas and righteousness. You'll become more and more isolated, alone and left out of life. You might feel godly as you look down on others from your high tower, or you may just feel cold living in your shadow of the fortress you built where no light nor love can linger. Your world will dim and new life become impossible.

Think of a lake covered in weed, starved of oxygen and sunlight.

Would you want to live with a belly like this, dark and slimy and full of critters and bugs? A gut without flowing water that's aired and full of life stagnates. The bowels cease to move, food decays and rots. This is not a prosperous environment for sure.

Emotions are a currency to be valued and adored. With the proper treatment your emotions will run clear, clean and vibrant, washing illness and decay from your body in a healthy stream of flowing energy. Emotions protect, cleanse and heal the body. They are your inner navigational system and the currency in your relationships. Emotions are the language of the Earth and the translator for Spirit.

Loving your anger will restore your integrity and harmony. You will gain the wisdom of the anger and be able to grow because of it, as the emotions begin to flow again.

Emotions respond directly to thoughts the way that the ocean responds to the wind and air pressure. Too much pressure in the mind will make clouds. Cloud block clear thinking. Emotional build up adds water which turns the clouds black and heavy, full of un-shed tears. You can't see in this weather. You need to rely on your other navigational instruments of feeling and sensing to go forward whilst doing some cloud busting.

With your mind clouded over and stormy, your emotions are in turmoil. The waters go dark with at the lack of light. With the attention up in the head, you are top heavy and unbalanced. When awareness is absent from the body stress builds up. Your unhappy, unloved, needy feelings come up, rising inside you, demanding attention, so that they can return and settle back down into the flowing rivers they belong in.

Settling your emotions is like soothing a child. Yelling at a child, telling them to man-up, shut up, or toughen up closes the doors tighter, blocking out even more light and oxygen. We need to learn to speak to our emotional selves with love and kindness, compassion and empathy, as we talked about in step 3 - Acknowledgment. Breathe from the mouth, as if holding the oxygen mask to your inner child. Allow the air to go deep into the epicentre of the emotion and expand it open. Gently speak to your emotions with respect.

It's a big problem that we just don't understand the value of our emotions. Perhaps like water we totally overlook it's preciousness because we have an abundance of it. But a world without water? A life without feeling? Yuk. Water is magic. It is the spirit of life in this world. I could write a whole book just about how amazing water is, and how amazing your breath is and still never capture the miracle.

Loving yourself entails valuing your emotional body, the water in you, the baby you in the watery womb world, the sensitive little inner child in you who spent the formative years of life on earth absorbing other people's feelings in empathy. When you love yourself enough, you go back, get on your knees and beg the little you to give up holding all that stuff. You look in their eyes and see the magic, the innocence and the beauty in you. You choose to stand by yourself no matter what and never let this child in you suffer again. You hold your inner child and love him or her until they feel safe again. Then they grow strong. Then they learn to have faith in you and trust you again. And guess what that means? It means you learn to trust your feelings, your intuition, and the ancient inner wisdom in you, presented as your inner child. She is the seer and sage. He is the guru who needs your devotion. Your child knows the route to joy, if you give them half a chance to speak, listen carefully and follow. Your life will change course as you follow your natural path.

Listen to your emotions as if it were the voice of your kindest mother, the Mother Earth herself. If your emotions aren't happy it means your Great Mother is telling you to come back into flow, come back into trust, that she has you, that you are loved, and that when you let go of whatever ails, fails or blocks you, the wisdom will become clear. The knowing will resurface and clarity will be your playmate again. Learn to empathise with yourself, accepting all that you feel as valid and real.

Love Your Body - You Matter

Your body is the densest possible substance, on the planet and in this known universe, that can deny knowing itself and be asleep, and yet enlighten and become conscious of all that it is. It is light compressed into the smallest of particles to appear heavy and solid. It takes a huge amount of resistance to stop these teeny particles from popping open and releasing the vastness of their light, and likewise a great deal of magnetism. Like a seed held in a shell, like an acorn in its case, like the energy stored inside every atom that's enough to blow up the world; like this are you.

The smallest particles of matter are called adamantine particles. Its where life begins and ends, they are the constant in everything in the universe.

(Perhaps that's why the first human was apparently called Adam?)

"Luminous beings are we, not this crude matter"
— Yoda, 'The Empire Strikes Back'

Mary Mageau — Author, describes it well:

"Adamantine particles describe all fundamental, subatomic particles. These particles form all of the elements in the universe by assembling the atoms of all the original substances such as oxygen, hydrogen, iron, etc. They are the basis of everything that exists, including our bodies and are the smallest particles that cannot be divided any further. Quantum physicists have already discovered these particles but have selected other names by which to identify them: electrons, quarks, muons, neutrinos etc. These pure particles are so small and simple that they represent an absolute and so are one of the constants of the universe. Adamantine particles are crystalline particles of infinity that all contain the stored potential to manifest any original substance or element. These particles are encoded with a type of universal 'DNA' somewhat like stem cells, which allow the particles to form any possible type of atom.

The Power of Love

> *Adamantine particles require power to build other particles and atoms. However, only one other type of energy is compatible with them. This energy is the magnetic power of love, which pervades the universe in the form of the Universal Life force, or Chi. Ki, Prana etc. Love is not only a most beautiful feeling, but is the power which ignites and directs adamantine particles into manifestation."*

— spiritualharmonics.blogspot.co.uk

Mary's article on adamantine particles and the relationship between it and love perfectly describes what I witness within the atoms of our human bodies. The outer casing of an atom is resistance, which holds it as a seemingly separate entity which can interact with other atoms to create and build matter. Resistance is a force that works apparently against us for a profound and meaningful reason, to hold atoms and matter in form. But within each atom is light particles in relationship with one another. When we breath and receive the breath of life itself into the cells, and into the atoms, they open like a corn popping in a heated pan. They unfurl like a baby fern, they reveal the true nature of our being; an infinite source of light. Our breath knocks upon the door, asking to bring us to the threshold of this experience. Receiving and feeling the infinite love energy or Prana of breath permits our entrance into this inner reality. Love opens us, opens the cellular and atomic doorways, allowing the light out, emitting into our bodies and lighting up our world. We enter the inner kingdom/queendom of life's brightest secret. Love is the very essence of our matter and yet, when we use our consciousness to see our true nature, its beauty makes us fall in love, and our love switches on the hidden potential. Consciousness is the conduit for love to enter matter and illuminate us, like "open sesame."

What Does This Mean?

It means that when you receive your breath into every particle of your body, dropping in and being aware of the kiss of life that touches every part of you in every moment, automatically given and nothing demanded in return, then you will see miracles.

Miracles!

When you notice that your body is an expression of unconditional love, squashed into a dense form so that you can wear it like a suit for your soul to walk around in, you might fall in love with the magic of it. You might choose to stop, breathe and feel it, and notice what a gift this body is. It is carved from the infinite substance. It is the very soil and substance of the earth itself, sculpted from her nutrient rich clay and made into a house for your spirit to breathe life into. All this is happening whether you notice it or not, the earth still turns the breath still comes. Life happens whether you recognise it's offering that it creates and is. BUT, when you do, when you take a drop of your consciousness and behold the inconceivable magic, the mystery is no longer a mystery. The movement of the stars is revealed in the microcosm of your cells. You will see God. You will see the Goddess. Both masculine and feminine qualities, existing and dancing as one yet standing apart like the pillars of the temple holding space for you, dear child, to play and be in wonder. Your matter, matters. It's really something special.

You Can Heal Yourself

No shadow exists in light, no gremlin can come out in the day. Loss, death, decay and darkness cannot abide in love. Take your ability to love by tapping into the source within your heart and breathe that love to any part of your body that is in decline. Breathe deep into the very cells, let the breath guide and show you the way to the door of your atoms. Surrender to the life that pours upon you in every moment and remember is it Love itself that beckons you to receive and 'be breathed'.

Receive the breath. Receive the love. See it. Witness it. Open your eyes to the sight within. Be willing to be revealed and your concepts blown. Be willing to gaze in wonder at the magnificence that is your atomic cluster like stars in the night sky. And when the door gives way, fall inside and be; breathing in the love that you are. Your cells will not stay sick for long. Receive true-love's kiss of life and turn back from a toad to what you once were, pristine and youthful and pure.

Love Everything.

Now, if that's all too abstract and cosmic for you, here it is again:

"Life Energy or Prana is all around us. It is pervasive;
we are actually in an ocean of Life Energy.
Based on this principle, a healer can draw in Pranic Energy
or Life Energy from the surroundings."
— Grandmaster Choa Kok Sui, the developer of Pranic Healing

Do This Now

Bring your hands to your body, anywhere that feels good to hold. Use your touch to acknowledge the parts and places that want to be seen, that are calling urgently your attention with pain.

Open your mouth and throat like a funnel for divinity to pour like liquid love into your vessel. Soften everything inside. Let the inner walls melt. Breathe and Receive breathe into the place that you want to bring healing or love to.

Let it go right to the heart of it. Close your eyes and watch what happens as you allow your breath into the density of your blockage, pain or problem.

Allow opening to happen. Surrender. Humble. Let go, forgive yourself for not yielding if you need to.

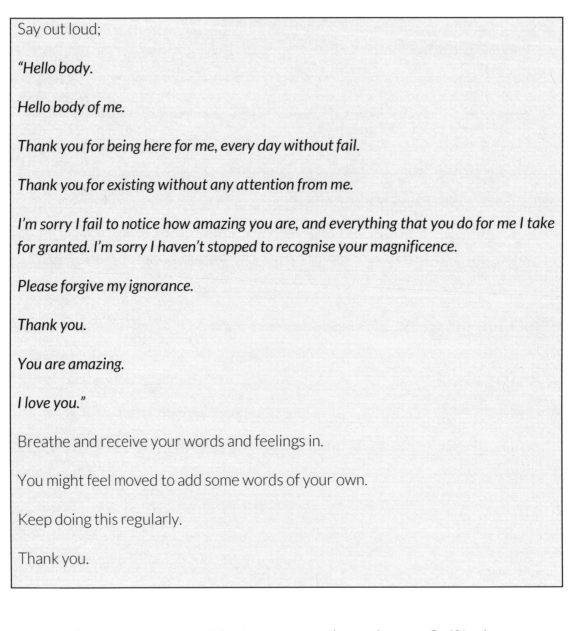

Say out loud;

"Hello body.

Hello body of me.

Thank you for being here for me, every day without fail.

Thank you for existing without any attention from me.

I'm sorry I fail to notice how amazing you are, and everything that you do for me I take for granted. I'm sorry I haven't stopped to recognise your magnificence.

Please forgive my ignorance.

Thank you.

You are amazing.

I love you."

Breathe and receive your words and feelings in.

You might feel moved to add some words of your own.

Keep doing this regularly.

Thank you.

Love your shadow. Love your quirks. Love your moles and warts. Or if it pleases you, love yourself by removing them. Please yourself in the morning with your favourite breakfast (mine is raw chocolate smoothie with a concoction of magical super food powers and potions, fruits and a splurge of maple syrup).

Love your body with a stroke and a stretch, a run or a leap or a bounce on the bed.

Love yourself by how long you sleep. Love yourself by keeping a reliable rhythm. Love yourself by remembering that it's a gift to have received You this morning when you woke up. The present of this moment was right there waiting at your door, the moment your Me became conscious again.

"Hello me! I love you, me! Thank you for being here again, me"

Love yourself in all your dirt and blood and bones, needs and desires, carnal and pure. Love yourself and your face will lift without botox and radiate a smile of one who is adored.

Love yourself in the afternoon with a little less coffee and a bit more play to get you through the day. Love your mischief, your humour, your idiosyncratic one-line bloomers. Love your gut so it digests happily instead of struggling and suffering under all your self-disgust. Love your feet and give them a rest. Love your mind and to thine own self be kind. Being ashamed causes all your pain.

Love yourself at dinner by cooking up a yummy winner. Be in pleasure. Eat with joy or not at all. Love yourself in bed at night, and wrap your arms around yourself tight. Love yourself in **all** of the places, misdemeanours, fails and hidden, dreaded spaces. "I love you me!"

Being good won't make you be loved,
but love will make you feel good!

Loving Reminder

- STEP 5-
I LOVE MYSELF ENOUGH TO LOVE EVERYTHING

❖   I Love Everything in me that needs, wants and deserves to be loved.

❖   Everything I am is love, either found and realised or hidden and waiting to be uncovered.

❖   Am I loving myself right now?

❖   How could I love myself more in this moment?

❖   If I loved myself enough, what would I be willing to choose instead?

❖   If I was the kindest, most perfect mum or dad, what would I give to my little me right now?

❖   If I was the, oldest, wisest, most pure and divine being, what would I tell myself to do right now?

❖   I have an unlimited well of unconditional love within me to drink from to feel whole and good.

❖   The more harmony I bring to my own life the more I resonate with a truth, beauty, clarity and joy that affects the whole world.

❖   Everything of me was made by and exists because of a loving creative source.

❖   Everything about me needs to be loved and is worth loving.

❖   Truth feels good. I trust that the better it feels the more true it is.

❖   Everything of this world gets left this side of the veil. Love is the only thing we can take with us.

Tara Trilogy ~ Part 3

I've wanted to die so many times in my life, simply because I didn't feel loved enough. It sounds awful but it's true. I don't always feel like that, just once in a while. The last time I felt like that **was** the last time, for a reason. I changed it. I managed to change a very deep seated, painful belief that had seemed true, that I couldn't even remember the origin of, nor rationalise with, nor heal no matter what else I did or didn't do. Even though I surely know that I'm loved by life, my parents, my kids, my friends and my past partners, and probably more people than I even know, I had felt ultimately unloved and on dark nights of the soul had wanted to leave the world until I did this:

The love of my life, the man who I'd been with for the past five years and who had wanted to marry me, changed his mind. Being an adventurer, he'd gone to Western Australia to find gold; a life-long dream of his. Upon his arrival in WA he Skyped me to say that he wanted to make the gold he intended to find into a wedding ring that no other person had ever touched. He wanted it to be pure, and to give it to me. He told me it would be the best thing he'd ever done in his life; to marry me. I didn't take it too seriously. I know he's a commitment phobe.

He texted me a few weeks later with a photo of himself holding a lump of gold saying, "Get ready for a wedding." The following five months while he was away we talked it over on the phone. I looked at dresses and venues, ecstatically in my joy. He hunted for more gold. I also spent a whole month with him adventuring in the outback, all the while we were blissful and in love.

However, when he returned home after nearly seven months of being away, he brought a dark cloud with him. He quickly became depressed, scared, angry and distant. He was difficult to communicate with and intimacy stopped. Then, over the smallest misunderstanding he moved into the spare room, and stayed there for two months with barely sight or sound from him. I deduced that the relationship was over and the wedding off. I was devastated. It wasn't just the rug that was pulled from beneath my feet, it was the walls and the ceiling and the floor too.

Words like "But I thought..." and "But I believed him when..." circled like vultures round and round my head, picking my sanity to pieces. I found myself staring down a black hole, an abyss was sucking me in. My mind was out of control trying to figure out "why?" The pain was eating into my heart and my womb, the grief filling my lungs and my eyes. My soul and mind were ravished and distraught. I now understood why people actually kill themselves when their lover leaves them, something I had previously thought was too extreme, a bit over-dramatic and pointless. Of course, my love for my children meant that I couldn't really take my life. I would never do that to them, what kind of example would I be if I did that?

I asked myself the questions, "Am I loving myself right now?" Answer, "No."

"Would I be willing to love myself enough to stop my pain and suffering?" Answer, "No!!!!"

I was surprised. Shocked that my answer was not a "Yes, of course I love myself enough." After all, I am The 'I love you me lady'.

I said, "Hello Me that doesn't want to love myself enough" and then I found her, a little me, hiding down a deep well inside me. She said she didn't know what it felt like to be loved unconditionally, with no guilt, strings, expectations, or judgements, or wanting anything in return attached. She said she'd never seen it and couldn't relate. She said she'd rather keep the pain which still felt like love, even though it wasn't. It was better than nothing.

I said, "Bless you little me, I'm sorry that you've never been loved and you don't know what true love is..." and some other empathising words that hit the nail on the head for her. She felt seen. She felt heard. I said I loved her enough to not let her be in pain and want to die, and that I would love her unconditionally. "Please forgive me" made her let go of the pain. "I love you" made her see that there is such a thing as love absolute. She came home. I got her back. She never looked down again, and I stopped smoking my ritual one native American Spirit ('cos that makes it better and more spiritual to smoke, wink, wink!) hand rolled cigarette a day; a twenty-two and a half year habit. It happened automatically. My addiction to painful love ended and so did my addiction to smoking, just like that.

I had a couple of bouts of growing pains afterwards though, and a few more layers to let go of as I climbed out of that deep, dark inner 'no-one really loves me and therefore life isn't worth living' pit. But, really I was healed within weeks. Now I am a queen. My magnetism to people who can't or won't love me is neutralised and reversed. I attract so much love it's wonderful. I watch how a different calibre of men arrive into my life, those who are strong of heart and able to love. I reversed a trend. I magnetise my love match, not my pain match. It is revolutionary!

Until I learned to love myself enough, I felt life's invisible love for me. During times of feeling suicidal as a teenager, before I had my own children as a reason to stay, I felt Life pull me from the pit. Something in me said, 'Stay. It's not all as it seems, just you wait.' I had faith in true love being a thing and not just a fairy tale. I didn't know it would be me that I had to learn to love, and me whom I eventually fell in love with; and, that's not narcissism, that's profound; that's life altering.

*"Darkness is not a presence. It is just the absence of light.
Cruelty is not a presence. It's just the absence of kindness.
Pain is not a presence. It's just the absence of joy.
Suffering is not a presence.
It's just the absence of peace."*
—Prem Rawat

True Stories

"The love of my life didn't want to COMMIT. And the more I planned, manipulated and eventually FORCED him, the more he would hide under a rock and distance himself from me. A little further away every day, for years. Why did I take that so PERSONALLY and start interpreting it as a major act of abandonment?

Never did I realise this might be an issue for <u>him</u> to overcome which would very likely play itself out with other females as well.

Nope, I made it all about <u>me</u>. That I was unlovable, not 'worth' committing to and that every man would eventually abandon me. Just like my father did when he suddenly died.

Friends got worried about how deeply I took this burden on. Over the years I seemed to be sinking deeper and deeper and I lost my glow and lively eyes.

My Facebook posts became that of an angry spinster. A bitter 42 year old who hated her ex and men in general.

Then one day, I looked in the mirror. My self-belief had become so ingrained, that I didn't recognise the person anymore that I was staring at. I was looking at an empty shell. If that shell was empty, then where was <u>I</u>? Where was <u>I</u> hiding? If it wasn't in my body, then clearly <u>I</u> had abandoned me too!

That is when I contacted Tara Love Perry and asked her to help find <u>me</u> back. I was in Australia at the time and on a warm spring evening she appeared on Skype. She started initiating her process and I remember thinking: 'How is this going to help?'

But something inside of me told me to keep going with it. Surrender to the process. Be pro-active. So I did.

During that evening I experienced how hard I found it to tell <u>me</u> that I loved me. It started off with just words that meant nothing but as the hours progressed, those words starting <u>hitting me.</u> They were suddenly resonating within my body and as we travelled through all the parts that were abandoned, I truly realised that it wasn't my ex-partner that had abandoned me. That nobody from the outside can abandon me unless I had already abandoned me.

That if I had truly LOVED me, over the course of the years I could have chosen to:

1. *Accept my big love didn't want to commit and therefore visualise and find someone who <u>was</u> available.*

2. *Or: Accept that my big love didn't want to commit and love him for what he <u>was</u> able to give.*

After my session with Tara I became very aware of mind patterns I was in that were keeping me in a loop of painful thoughts. I understood that the 'I Love You, Me' process was an ongoing one that I could apply every time an old thought pattern would come up. And I did.

I thought 'if I can extend that way of looking at life and apply it to my ex, then I am truly well on the way.'

And lo and behold he contacted me the next day. We decided to meet and chat.

Normally a meeting between us would end up in bed, but not this time.

I asked questions about how <u>he</u> felt in life about things. I listened to him. And as I did I realised how his own lack of self-love created such a fear of abandonment which he prevented from ever actualising by simply never committing.

And while the attraction between us was sizzling as ever, I truly felt that my body was too sacred and special to be used casually.

I now loved myself enough to wait for the man to come along, who like me, was ready to start loving himself.

Today, I am responsible for the fun life I have. I make choices every day between self-sabotage or mindfulness and conscious intent. And the more I choose the latter, the more my mind rewires. And the more that happens, the more my body enjoys being alive. I say 'yes' to a fun night out. Because I love me and therefore I deserve fun. I say 'no' to a job that doesn't inspire me even though the money would be great. Because I love me and therefore I don't do jobs that prove the opposite.

Another great effect of the 'I Love You, Me' process is that suddenly the work that I am meant to be doing presents itself <u>through</u> me. Rather than <u>me</u> looking externally for the next job, it just happens through me. I am inside of me and everything is birthed inside of me.

And you know what's funny? I am happy being single now. Not that I wouldn't want to be with someone as well, but I am with me, first and foremost."

—Christianne van Wijk, Filmmaker

Step 6
Magnitude of Gratitude

LOVING YOURSELF ENOUGH TO SHOW SELF-APPRECIATION

Gratitude Makes You Great!

You've probably heard of The Attitude of Gratitude. It's based on the premise that being grateful for what you already have, generates an abundance of having more. Gratitude is the highest state of emotion a human being can have. In gratitude we can experience true bliss. Gratitude opens doorways to the inner realms of the heart in the same way that a rose opens petal after petal until it is in fullest bloom. Gratitude has no limits.

Here's the golden nugget...

Saying, 'Thank you, Me' completes the cycle, it ties up all loose ends and makes everything that you've just acknowledged, forgiven and loved a 'done-deal'. When we have asked for something with a "Please forgive me" saying thank you signs the contact. We were taught to say, 'thank you' after we were given what we wanted. After the 'please,' there often comes a long, slow, sometimes painful, wait to get it. The Thank you is delayed. We may pray, beg and bargain but the deal is still open for negotiation. It is incomplete. Saying Thank you is an out loud affirmation that you are ready to receive, that it IS being given, that it IS coming and that the deal is finalised.

How does it feel when you say, "Thank you" after saying please? Does it feel real? Are you having to imagine or is there something tangible, more solid than wishful thinking or visualisation? If you can say, 'thank you,' breath it in, and feel it to be digestible and satisfying, then your mind is free from clinging on to the wish or "plea-plea-please can I have?" mentality.

Thank You, Me!

We want people to say, 'thank you' to us when we do something of value, give a service or make effort towards them. We get gratification from giving, and yet it can feel as if they did not receive our giving until they acknowledged us with a 'Thank you'. Some of us give and give and give, but no thank you's come back to us for it. Has our giving gone unnoticed? Was our giving valuable? We can feel left out of the picture and sometimes feel overlooked, undervalued and unacknowledged when appreciation is not shown to us.

If you're a person who generously dishes out 'Thank you's to people, giving positivity and gratitude because you understand the power of acknowledging others, ask yourself how many 'Thank you's have you given to yourself lately for all your giving?

Thank you for being here, right now. Thank you for coming this far in this book, thank you for listening and trusting me. Thank you for doing all the good work you do, and for giving all that you give to others.

I'm sorry that sometimes, or often, you feel unrecognised or unacknowledged for your giving. Please forgive me. Please forgive us that we forget to be grateful and extend out acknowledgment to you. I love you. Thank you, for being the warm generous person you are. Thank you for being loving, and kind and for wanting to help people.

I'm sorry that the help has sometimes not felt reciprocated and that you've been alone doing so much. Please forgive me that you sometimes do not get the help you need, or feel, that you deserve. I love you. Thank you for receiving me now. Thank you for receiving this acknowledgment and being kind and generous enough to let me give back to you, to taste your own medicine. Please now give the medicine to yourself on a daily basis because you need it. We all need you to be, and feel, extortionately loved and appreciated, so that you shine in the world. We need you to feel happy, healthy wealthy and supreme in your being, for the highest good of the planet, as an example, as the leader that you are, as the game changer, healer, leading edge of humanity and paradigm shifter that you are!

Thank you for everything that you do to make a difference and contribute. Thank you for daring to be yourself, to be authentic, to be real, Thank you for loving unconditionally and thank you for now choosing to love yourself, your Me, inclusively.

We all need you to be included too. It does not serve anyone to try to serve one another from a place of **conditional** love. We give what we get, and we often give ourselves such a hard time that when we think we're giving to others they often miss it, feeling instead the energy that you give yourself. Your conditional self-love emits from you, and despite being kind and good, your conditions will be felt by others. They may feel that you are giving them a hard time too, because it's how you treat yourself. It's true! Think about it.

Think about the people with whom you try most hard to please. Do they feel given to? Or do they get angry and displeased and ask for more, or tell you that what you do for them is not good enough?

See!

Reverse the process. Undo your conditional giving, because really we give all of ourselves to be loved back, even if we just get crumbs of love back instead of the full hearted meal. Faking satisfaction with crumbs will leave you ill, disillusioned, lethargic and low. You're all given out and it just doesn't make sense, does it? So, take this ability you have to be generous, kind, giving and loving, being attentive to details and considerate, and first consider that the giver needs to be FULL.

Conditional giving begets conditional receiving.

Many cultures and religions of the world preach that we must first feed our neighbour. We think that is beautiful and good of us to do so. We think that we can go without, that it makes us a better person; better to be giving than selfish — right? Are selfish people loving themselves? Or do they perhaps feel such hatred for themselves and so sorely missing the love, that they have become consumers — eating, buying, stealing, sapping every little bit of energy they can get to fill themselves because they did not choose to fulfil themselves first?

When we are full, we automatically seek to serve and give to others.

When you've had your fill at dinner, you have energy to feed many others. When you have a full bank account, it's easy to donate money to a worthy cause and feel great about it. If everyone served themselves first with the food of unconditional love, wouldn't we each learn what unconditional love really looks and feels like? The love we feel would be authentic, therefore the love we give would be authentic. When we serve our heart, we serve the world. We raise the bar on Love by adding a concentrated dose of our own, into the soup of displacement, confusion and sadness surrounding us.

When we are full we can be truly great-full. Overflowing! Abundant!

Gratitude is Expansive. It will expand your capacity to receive, expand your perceptual horizons, and expand what you are now capable of giving. And when you are full, the gratitude comes easy. Not like putting a sticking plaster on a wound to make the pain of emptiness go away, and not like slapping a thick layer of icing over an unpalatable cake of your life to make it sweeter. Saying, 'thank you' is the delicious recognition that you *are all*, that you *have all*, and are *becoming all* that you will ever need or want.

Gratitude Seals The Deal

Gratitude is the bookend to a request. We ask for something with a "Please," and after we've received, it's polite to say, "Thank you." It's rarely recognised, but 'thank you' is so much more than just a polite expression.

'Thank you' is the perfect way to acknowledge that, where there was a want, the want has been fulfilled. What was asked for was given. The hunger was satiated, the thirst quenched, the roof provided - The need is met - Thank you.

So, where we are asking for something that we don't yet have, where there is an apparent 'lack', we say "Please..."

"Please forgive me," (Release me, I have a lack of freedom and harmony), "Please can I have…"(I am lacking something),

"Please will you…"(do something that I need and don't yet have).

The resonance of please is that of needing, lack and longing. After saying please we usually have a waiting period, whether it be seconds, minutes, hours, weeks, or years. Maybe even life-times, as the 'please' rings on and on, infinitely out into the universe like ripples on an infinite lake. We wait for our pleas to be answered, our requests to be granted, our prayers heard.

For example, if we are asking for money because we don't have enough; we are in lack. We have our hand outstretched begging, please universe, give me more money…the signal of lack goes out…the asking… the energy of begging ripples into the future…you send a signal of lack. Someone notices and feels pity for your lack…they vibe with you. They could put a money note into your hand, and for a moment your poverty will feel recognised. You say thank you because your lack was noticed. Maybe you made them feel inadvertently guilty. But you still experience lack. You ask again, you are given, you feel grateful. But for what? Having your emptiness witnessed? Making others feel sorry for you?

You are basically saying, "Please see that I am poor… thank you for seeing that I am poor"

Your focus is on the lack, and you ask for more. This kind of thank you perpetuates the lack. It is a response to the lack. Thank you seals the deal. You are cementing in your lack. No amount of money will ever fill your begging bowl because it has a hole. Your low self-worth, habit of feeling poverty and the emptiness that lack brings you is sustained because you appreciate that people see your condition.

We get more of what we say 'Thank You' for.

Until this happens:

Notice the difference now: You feel poverty. You notice that this feeling of poverty doesn't feel 'good,' it's out of harmony with you. It doesn't feel like it's your truth, yet that's what seems real in this moment. You're trapped in it. You decide to transform it with the steps shown so far, so that your self-worth pattern is released and the hole is filled with self-love. After saying sorry to poor you, forgiving poor you and loving poor you, a natural gratitude arises. You have chosen to independently take care of your needs and love yourself enough to ask for help to get stronger.

You put out your bowl and effectively ask, "Please help me to help myself. Thank you for helping me to help myself. I love myself enough to be given to and receive the wealth. Thank you for recognising this worthiness in me," before a single coin is dropped. By the time these words are spoken, what you feel is gratitude for your prayers already being answered. It's a done deal. You feel worthy of being given to. You value yourself enough to truly receive what benevolence comes. You already feel rich, not poor and empty. You now feel connected to life's abundant stream again, not separate and alone. It's a done deal. It's only a matter of time before you become tangibly rich.

You transmuted. Gratitude arises in you like the fragrance from an orange blossom bud opening to the spring, no longer closed and withholding its beauty. Love makes things blossom, and gratitude is the fragrance that emanates from the blossom — it's for savouring. Then when we say thank you, it's for the resurrection of what was buried. We can honestly say thank you for the illusion being dispelled, for our true nature being restored. We can say thank you for the transformation that has taken place, and our gratitude can be a celebration of the love that conquered the darkness of our not-knowing, delusional, ignorant, naïve, or innocent thinking. And gratitude grows and expands giving us MORE of what we feel grateful for. In this case, we receive an abundance of restoration from poverty, the harmony of abundance and healthy wealth, and not an abundance of poverty repeating.

Let's say that the beggar held out his hands and repeatedly said "Thank you" and was given a lot of money because he said thank you *for the money.* Because of the law that says we get more of what we say thank you for, like attracts like, one-day he becomes wealthy. By trying to fill his empty bowl he now has a lot of money. Is his beggar bowl full? Does he still feel empty? Is the money fulfilling him, does he have enough?

The likelihood of him feeling the emptiness within himself, no matter how much money he gets, is high. The poverty would still reside in his heart as if it were the truth, one day returning the beggar to poverty again because that's who he believes he is. And if he doesn't love himself enough to be wealthy and live in a naturally abundant state, he will lose every penny that's ever given to him. He's a bucket with a hole.

A person must decide to transform from the core. No amount of external decoration can hide us from the facts of what we feel fundamentally lacking in. We can know something in the ego know-it-all mind, and yet not feel it. We can know that we deserve everything cognitively and rationally, and yet fail to actually feel the depth of it within us.

Would you be willing to love yourself enough to become wealthy — in every area of your life, not just money?

Thank you seals the deal, according to what we internally feel.

Thank you me for recognising my areas of lack

and thank you for choosing to fulfil them.

Thank you me for noticing my poor me,

and thank you me for no longer being poor.

Thank you me for understanding my humbling needs,

and thank you me for being kind enough to give to me.

Please is asking, thank you is receiving.

Love is what happens in between.

> **Please now go to Step 6 Exercise 1 in your workbook to complete the transformation process on what you've already asked to change in your life.**
>
> **~ Thank you!**

Acknowledgment Of Harmony

As well as 'Thank you' being the most perfect words to acknowledge what will be, is, and has been given, 'Thank you' is also the most powerful way to acknowledge what *is in harmony with you,* (as opposed to 'Sorry' being the perfect acknowledgment for what's *out of harmony).*

Sorry for what doesn't feel good. Thank you for what does.

Sorry for what you lack. Thank you for what you have.

Sorry for what doesn't serve you, thank you for what does.

These steps of 1) Connect within, 2) Decision, 3) Acknowledgment, 4) Release and 5) Love Everything, are a gardening process of turning the soil. Once aerated, cleansed, well composted and blessed, it is capable of rich and abundant fertility. It is ready to receive. Not much grows in a state of lack. Everything grows in a state of love. And when love is the state, true gratitude is the most compatible ally, blowing in like a touch of the divine and generating exponential growth.

Be grateful for what you have. Be sorry for what you don't have, then transform it until it's regained it's true state. Then be grateful for that. Gratitude is like an invisible angel. It can accompany you even into the darkest places and say thank you to the poor little impoverished you! Thank you for changing your state. Thank you for revealing the truth. Thank you for being willing to release what's not your truth. Thank you for finding the heart to love what you are, and what you are not. Thank you for loving everything. Under these conditions of unconditional gratitude, magnificent growth happens! The Magnitude of Gratitude! The deal is sealed. There's no going back.

What else can gratitude do?!

Gratitude, The Magnifier

Gratitude is an eye opener. When looking through the lens of appreciation it increases perception, brings something into focus like a magnifying glass. Noticing what's in harmony, what's beautiful, what works and what feels good, has the effect of opening the aperture of the third eye, as if it were a camera lens. Gratitude allows more light in for the subject to be observed. What IS can be seen more clearly. The practice of being grateful opens the inner eyes and increases our perceptual ability, so that we may again be wide eyed and in wonder like a child. Does gratitude expand and magnify the subject of our appreciation, or is it our own eyes that are widened, and vision more clearly focused? The wonderful mystery!

Quantum physics would have us believe that the effect of the observer changes the subject matter, since matter is merely particles of light. Their order can easily be rearranged according to how we choose it to be. If this is the case, then we are very powerful beings, with the ability to transform atomic structure according to our will; according to what we choose to perceive, as I described with love and adamantine particles.

Thankfully, true gratitude also requires a large dose of humility. For if we are masterful beings who can alter matter according to our will, then what kind of world would we live in if that will was directed by the mind driven, hunger driven, lack driven, egotistic desires? We don't have to look too far to see that already in action, and it's not pretty.

Without the force of love, what we create is ultimately destructive, both to one's self, and the rest of humanity. Humility opens the doors to love. That's why we breathe and say sorry first. Forgiveness can only happen when there's humility to let go and stop clinging or fighting or grabbing for what we think we want. Forgiveness humbles us enough to allow love to come in. And gratitude from a place of genuine humility is the most empowering thing one can feel, as a human being. It is illuminating. It inspires devotion. It inspires Bliss. It inspires an experience of what Hindus call 'Darshan' Or "Darshana'.

Poet Gary Snyder has given a naturalistic meaning to Darshana:

> "It's a gift; it's like there's a moment in which the thing is ready to let you see it. In India, this is called darshan. Darshan means getting a view, and if the clouds blow away, as they did once for me, and you get a view of the **Himalayas** from the foothills, an Indian person would say, 'Ah, the Himalayas are giving you their darshana'; they're letting you have their view. This comfortable, really deep way of getting a sense of something takes time. It doesn't show itself to you right away. It isn't even necessary to know the names of things the way a botanist would. It's more important to be aware of the 'suchness' of the thing; it's a reality. It's also a source of a certain kind of inspiration for creativity."

One of my most profound moments of gratitude-inspired bliss was when I gave birth to my fist child. My awareness was in total light. I was in such a state of sublime ecstasy, a completely open channel for receiving the spirit of creation through my body to deliver my son's soul to this earth, that I actually named him Darshan. This is the energy in which he was born, so you can imagine what a powerful presence he is!

It is only with humility and surrender that this state of birth was achieved. I was first filled with the state of love for the energy moving through me, then I had to let go even more to receive the full state of gratitude for that love. Gratitude completed a magnificent process. This birth is another story... one which you shall hear in due course and the story will be available for you to read. But I'm telling you now because it opened my eyes. I had profound realisations as to what was experientially achievable in this human body. I understood that humble surrender to Love and Gratitude yields existential occurrences. It bonds a seemingly separate being, an entity such as this 'Me,' back into union with Divinity. It dissolves obscuring clouds of thought and mind and limited belief and opens the eyes to the heavenly, mountainous reality of 'Suchness', as Gary Snyder puts it.

Gratitude opens the eyes, because when we see the harmony that exists in every living thing, person or situation, it sharpens our focus to look around and see more of the same. Whatever we perceive with the outer eyes, and formulate from it, sends commands to the pituitary gland in the centre of the forehead, between the eyes. It then reads the signals, deciphers the chemical dosage for hormone production, and disperses them around the body. So, if for example, we experience a situation as safe, warm and loving, the pituitary excretes the chemical to produce melatonin, to produce oxytocin which relaxes the body and allows a deepening of intimacy.

It also sends an electrical current to the pineal which signals the third eye to open too, like an aperture on an old camera lens, to allow in more light, more colour frequencies within that light and then, as the inner eye opens further, to see new horizons, new worlds, new paradigms that are invisible to the closed off heart and mind. For instance, You don't have to believe in angels to see them, you have to be open to seeing whatever IS, and then believe in your eyes and inner senses! Magic appears where others see nothing special.

Gratitude opens the other senses, because all sensory organs and abilities are linked back to the pineal. It's the hub of the wheel if you like, and the senses are the spokes radiating out in their unique directions, like antenna, to collect information to relay back to head office.

All roads lead to God they say, and all sensory tracts lead to the 'God-head,' the seat of the Divine in the centre of the mind.

Appreciation is a tonic.

Appreciation is a polish, a beautifier, bringing a flush of warmth to the cheeks and a glow to the heart. Without appreciation, we wither and fade, often becoming gnarled and bitter, and twisted with resentment for never having had the sunlight shine upon us. Appreciation is a fundamental need. It doesn't just say, "I see you" it says, "I approve of you," thereby encouraging a person to continue boldly on with a swagger in their gait and confidence under their belt. It's a verification of our efforts and qualities that is crucial if we are to have fervour to endeavour and pursue our talents, creativity and purpose. To appreciate is to admire, and admiration, i.e., the ability to see/hear/feel/sense/smell/taste/touch beauty and harmony, is a tonic for the heart. It heals. It restores. It revitalises the wounded soul.

Thank You, Me

The perfect verbal expression of gratitude (at least in the English language) is "Thank you."

Gratitude opens the heart, taking one into deeper experiences of awakening, self-knowledge and Truth.

Appreciation for oneself is the highest honour we could give to Source, for we are Sources greatest gift to us. Thank you, for me, and thank you, me for recognising this gift as beautiful. When I appreciate myself, I need no other appreciation from others and feel full of appreciation to give. Appreciation gives peace and a sense of completion; no longer is there a need to seek validation.

After all that self-love, would you now be willing to love yourself more and interrupt your battering ram of heavy self-depreciation, offer up some tea and empathy, and invite your grateful-self to the party?

How does it feel when someone genuinely appreciates you? Finally! It's like someone's noticed what **you've been noticing** all along. It's validation of your efforts. It's validation of your existence.

People wait their whole lives to be appreciated, especially those who like to give a lot. Giving makes them feel good, makes them feel significant, slightly saintly even. But the trouble with giving, as we have already discovered in previous chapters, is that by itself, it's not sustainable. The other side of giving, in alignment with the dualistic nature of humanity and earthy life, is receiving. If we, as separate-seeming entities, with our separate bodies and separate lives, are constantly attempting to give something of ourselves to another, it drains our battery. Our life force is lessened. When we are tapped in, tuned in, turned on to the Life Force steam of infinite and perpetual giving, being a RECEIVER, then we become the vessel or channel for Life to give to itself.

When we are full we naturally emit whatever we are full of, be it light, love, pain or bad vibes.

What do you want to be full of? What's your signature vibe?

Depreciating yourself is an insult to Creator.

In this endless stream of life giving to life, and giving back to life, we are the ones blessed with the pleasure of swimming amidst this stream, feeling its power and benevolence wash over us in every breath. When we appreciate what is being given however, we are not just washed and in flow, but something else magnificent happens. Our gratitude positively validates Life's efforts and existence, thereby *magnifying* the flow. It literally turns up the volume and intensity of life's generosity and benevolence!

Saying thank you to life is one thing, and life certainly appreciates the recognition. But when we appreciate the very specific and unique thing that life is creating for us, right here right now; this incredible vessel of consciousness that has been dreamt of, planned eons ago, and then manifested into existence; your 'Me,' then life really starts to celebrate!

"Thank you for 'ME!' and thank you me for recognising this beautiful gift. It is an honour to do everything I can to fully appreciate myself. I need no other appreciation from others because I can give it exactly where needed, and in my fullness of appreciation, I have an abundance to share."

Appreciation gives us peace and a sense of completion. The deal is sealed.

How Do You Appreciate Yourself?

Some say there's not much to appreciate. We aren't used to looking, so we fail to see. So, let's imagine you can see yourself through the eyes of someone who really loves you. If you can't think of anyone, try your God, or Idol, or an Angel.

What would you admire? Would the person who loves you say, 'You're so fat' on a daily basis, or "Gosh you're ugly," or "Wow, your bum is so horribly big," or "Man you're so stupid," or "Jees, you're such a bitch?" Or how about, "You can't afford that," or "Who do you think you are?" or "Do that impossible thing, jump this hurdle, prove your worth!"

Do you like it when people say stuff like that to you? Would you say that to your beloved? Course not. But you're okay with saying those sorts of things to yourself - EVERY DAY.

(NB If you said "yes" to any of those questions, go back and say "sorry me that you haven't been appreciated enough. Please forgive me that you've become judgemental and unkind from not being appreciated. I love you judgmental, unkind, unappreciated me." Thank you.)

You know, that when you say to someone, "well done" or "good job" they feel seen. They light up a little. You polished their inner glow lamp. It feels good to give it and see that smile. It sort of makes you happy, even though you gave it because somewhere deep down you need to receive it yourself, (we give what we long to get when we are unappreciated); even if the person you validated is hiding their smile, embarrassed to show their vulnerability. Some people don't want to let your acknowledgement in because they fear you've seen their poverty of appreciation. It's as if the need for it is a weakness, like their need for love.

To a person who hasn't had their needs validated or met, needs become a weakness. It's their Achilles heel. It's stronger not to need, or at least pretend. To a person whose self-appreciation is low or absent, you can pour on them all the gratitude you like, but it will run off in a puddle, like butter on a hot corncob. They will not let it in, they won't treat it as genuine and their resistant self-worthlessness will reverse magnetise it. It's a shame. You can lead a horse to water but you can't make it drink, so the old adage goes. Some people are too damaged that way. Perhaps you're one of them?

Why Would You Appreciate Yourself?

Perhaps you think it's vain to do so? Perhaps you don't want to inflate your own ego? Perhaps you think you don't need it? Perhaps you think it only works when coming from someone else?

Okay, what if you're right. Let's say you're a parent. I imagine you're a great parent and you give everything you can of yourself to your child or children, you sacrifice sleep, you work night and day, you go through the anguish of decision making, suffer the agony of watching them get hurt and be in pain with them, and you lavish them with all the attention and gifts you never got. What would recognition of your efforts do for you? I know you give it unconditionally and ask nothing in return, but what if I said thank you?

I genuinely mean this - Thank you for being such a great parent. Your efforts mean that you are helping to raise the next generation of loved, happy and empowered individuals for the betterment of their lives and the world. Thank you for giving of yourself so diligently, so selflessly. Thank you for doing your best, even if you think it isn't perfect enough (it will never be). Thank you for your love, your strength, your thoughtfulness. Well done for being such a wonderful parent. Well done for working your socks off, and well done for keeping going even when it gets tough. Good job! Thank you. I love you.

Has anyone ever said that to you before? If they have, you're lucky.

What about this — what about being appreciated for just being born?

I genuinely mean this too - Thank you for being here, in this body, in this life, still breathing. I know that it's been a hard road, not always easy, not always fun, but you're still here. Well done. Thank you for not leaving, or giving up, or dying just yet. Thank you for being born exactly as you are, perfect in your own way, special in your own unique and wonderful way. That you for all the efforts you make to give and love and share and be the best you can be. I appreciate that about you. I need you, we all need you, thank you.

Thank You, Me

Hmmm.... deep breath. How long must we wait, just like in all the other steps, for someone else to give us exactly the medicine we need, in exactly the right dosage to heal our longing hearts and aching bodies? Maybe my words didn't measure up exactly for you, how could you do it better? What do you wish I had said? Or maybe you wish a specific someone else had said those words instead?

How much longer do you want to wait in secret for the right one to appreciate you and notice what greatness you do? Another 5 years? 10 years? 20? Surely you love yourself enough by now to fill in your appreciation gaps and puff up your 'well done Me' chest, as your heart, not your ego, swells with the relief and joy of being seen. And to be honest, why not plump up your ego too. All parts of you need to feel good, why separate and judge? Just pour liberally. Butter yourself up!

Now please go to Step 6 Exercise 2 in your workbook to discover all the things you need to appreciate about yourself. Don't assume you already know this unless you've actually done this exercise. You will like it.

~ Thank you!

Well done.

Thanks for doing that. One more polished lamp in the world.

Loving Reminder

-STEP 6-
LOVING MYSELF MORE WITH THE MAGNITUDE OF GRATITUDE

- ❖ Next to love, and from the state of love, gratitude is the highest possible emotion I can experience.

- ❖ Gratitude causes me uncontrollable states of bliss, both emotionally and spiritually.

- ❖ Gratitude magnifies whatever I choose to focus on, bringing it into clearer focus and enhancing it.

- ❖ Appreciation opens my third eye like an old fashioned camera lens, or like the iris of the eye opens to allow more light in.

- ❖ 'Thank you' is the perfect way to acknowledge what is harmonious to me — the opposite and complimentary word to Sorry.

- ❖ Whenever I ask "Please," I say "Thank you" immediately afterwards to seal the deal. I receive in feeling, in the heart, and therefore in reality.

❖   Saying "Thank you," like sorry, requires my humility.

❖   Humility opens the door to my greatest empowerment — (Source/Heart based power, as opposed to ego/separation/fear based power).

❖   I am a master of manifesting and transformation, according to my perception. I can choose to see the lack or the love in everything, and therefore affect the material plane.

❖   When I transform my perception, natural gratitude arises. I cannot force gratitude because I think *I should.*

❖   When I am in Gratitude I receive more of what I want, and whatever else the universe has in flow to give me. It opens my Destiny.

❖   Appreciation is my fundamental need, to validate my efforts, qualities and existence.

❖   Approval encourages me to continue on, boldly and confidently, in my truth.

True Stories

"Before I worked with Tara I was very messed up physically, emotionally and spiritually. I had mental and physical health problems and was struggling financially. I prayed one day that a healer would come to help me solve what was going wrong in my life and that day I came across Tara's website and believed fate had brought me here. Tara's "I love you me" method taught me to forgive and let go of pain, hurt, suffering and the past, and be open to receiving goodness in my life. Tara also helped heal my inner child and childhood wounds and traumas. We also cleared a lot of negativity through my ancestral line. As a result of working with the "I love you me" method I have healed mental health problems an immune system problem, and bladder problems. I now have a lot more energy to do the things I love. My relationships with my family have improved. I have had success in my career as a script writer and healer, which was blocked before I met Tara. Mostly my relationship with myself has improved. I have learned to love and care for myself and to receive more. I found the hugging myself really hard at first because I've never been shown love in the past, but then I realised through the "I love you, me" method that it was because of this that I was now suffering. So now I do hug myself and love myself which has helped so much."

—Ash Khan, UK

"*I absolutely love this method.*

The first time I did the 'I love you, me' exercise with Tara, I was humbled, I felt like I was finally understood. It felt like a big embrace and a shower of acceptance and love onto me.

I remember sitting in nature, next to a little stream, pondering about some problem I had, and all of a sudden, I was doing Tara's I love you me exercise and really got down to the centre of my problem. It was deeply healing and deeply liberating. As I was sitting next to a little stream I could energetically let everything wash away.

Doing the "I love you me" during a live call with Tara was deeply healing, we worked on self-love and I was finally able to really accept myself just the way I am. A big shift happened then, and the sprout of Self Love is growing each day ever since.

Thank you Tara for all your awesome work and so honoured to be on this amazing journey with you. We can sure all do with "I love you me."

—Caroline Palmy - Heart Healer, UK

Step 7
Coming Home

I LOVE MYSELF ENOUGH TO COME BACK TO THE TRUTH

There's No Place Like Home

You'd be surprised how many people say, "I want to go home, I've had enough of this planet," whilst others may be slightly baffled. "Whadaya mean? Are you crazy, leave the planet???"

Well, yes.

Some people literally do mean that, as if they've come from somewhere else, far away, another dimension maybe, to be here, on this earth, in the shape of a human-being. Others are longing for a place they don't quite remember in their mind, but ache for in their heart; A place where they feel loved, contented, belonging, peaceful, able to be themselves; at home.

What Does Coming Home Mean?

When I say Come Home, I'm making a command or a request for every part of you that has gone off wandering, out there in the world or the stratosphere searching, and come up empty handed, to return. It's to say, when you've had enough of un-fulfilment and disillusionment, come back to what you forgot about. Come back to what you left behind. Come back to the innocent child within, that waited patiently while the grown-up in you, went out in search of food to feed your soul. Come back to the little one who's been abandoned, malnourished and recklessly uncared for.

Come back to your hearth, your heart, the light of your existence.

Come back to the Source, the safe place, the space that is stable.

Come back from perception to truth.

This place is within you; the place from where all life comes, and to where all life must eventually return. It's the beginning and the end of your journey, and the continuum of Now in every moment. It's inside your chest like a swirling mass of consciousness, and yet singular and still. We could say it is Divine, or we could call it nothing. It's the void and the fullness, the alpha and the omega, the formless and all-form. It IS.

And because it IS; You Are.

Here.

Right Now.

If you want to phone home, pick up the receiver and hear the voice from a place you have always known, but mostly forgotten.

It's your Soul Calling!

It's the Ocean of Souls that holds you close like a babe, and has never let you go. You have to feel it to believe it. For, like love, Creation eludes the tiny box made for mental conceptualisation. It is everything outside the box, and its game is LOVE; Big LOVE; Enormous, unending, indefinable, love. But it can only tell you about that if you listen, stay still and feel, deeply.

When you follow your breath, it delivers you to the door of this place. You have to go in empty headed.

And this is why we've done the journey; connecting, and getting back on track, acknowledging the out-of-synch, and plain out-of-order parts of your 'Me' machine. Then we bathed them with sorrys and washed them clean with forgiveness, and released back all the hurt to the great big mama of Life. Then, we diligently went around planting love seeds in the barren places, scooping up the sludge of composted years, and warming the coldest of your parts with love. Then we acknowledged the good work done with thank you and well done. We tidied up the loose ends and gave thanks for the courageous unraveling. So now here's the part where we summon into our arms all that was discarded as unholy; and left you feeling un-whole; and return it to the core of Creation; our Source, our one Universal Soul.

It's like going back to step 1, only now we're not starting off naive and in ignorance. We return to the beginning a new person; wiser and more knowing.

The home for your 'Me' is your body.

Some people have said that all life is 'Maya,' an illusion; that none of this earthy stuff of life is real. Therefore, they have pursued the Sun-God, or sought enlightenment in the out-of-reach realms that only a few may attain, (if they're good enough - Wink!) Nirvana is a place for the spiritual elite. To some, spirituality is everything, whilst the earth and body is nothing. Just dust; all temporary and not worth anything.

I found this very confusing as a child. Imagine being five years old and a being told by a grown up whom you trust, that everything on this earth, including our body isn't real. How would that make you feel about your existence? As I stated earlier, everything is energy and all particles of matter are made of light, and therefore not solid at all. But it could be construed as meaning that you, therefore, do not exist. That you are not real. You might interpret, as I did being five, that it meant there was no point to being in a body because it's not the truth of who I am. It put me off being in a body altogether; hence always wanting to leave.

Another spiritual philosophy, one we covered previously as well, is that to be incarnate into a human body, means you have sinned. Like being at the bottom of a ladder, you are now the lowest expression of God or Divinity and must ascend UP to heaven, to be good, godly, pure and therefore allowed into heaven. It's all been about ascension, up there, out there, away from where you are now. In meditation we are taught to let go of the body sensations, sit still, ignore the pain and become detached from our mortality. If we are 'here,' in a body, and yet the purpose is to somehow escape it, become spiritually better than it, or transmute it by focusing only on positivity and light, *then what's the point of having a body?* People talk about chakras, and how we have to move into our higher chakras, and be in our higher selves. But what about our lower ones, and our lower self? Is that worthless then? A mistake of the Creator?

What is a lotus without the root? What is the Sun without the Earth?

Bring your awareness, back from out there, to your body, here, in the physical. Many people don't like this. We reject our bodies, we reject this world as not good enough, and we resist being any part of it. But when we do, we come home. If you don't recognise your body as such, it's probably because you let others inhabit you; their thoughts, their feelings, their wants and needs. They crowded you out, took over, and dominated your 'me' space. You may have thought, 'get me outta here, I'm off to better lands and pastures greener'. Maybe you left your home, and your country, to find a better one that suited you more, and in doing so, you've chucked the baby out with the bath water; you left you.

If you let others dump their rubbish on you, then yes, you won't feel very homely. If you gave your body away to others to do with as they wish, you will feel homeless and have to reclaim it. If your body was stolen and taken by force, then you have some evicting to do, to get the thieves off your property and clean off their marks. As I said before, this is *your birthday present*, your soul's suit and your house to dwell in whilst you sojourn on earth. Don't let anyone ruin that for you.

Some people live only in the top floor, the control room mind, observing life from the high watch-tower. Imagine living in a light house. Or like Rapunzel in the fairy story, who was locked in the tower by the wicked witch, unable to get out. You'd feel so disconnected. I think we covered that already...

Some people live on the roof, unable to occupy even their own head, because it's so cramped with overwhelming stuff. Some people live way out there, in the realms of imagined realities and illusion, thinking so much is real when it's only a trick; a virtual reality, made of levels to 'win,' warlocks, aliens and enemies to be conquered, as if it's a never ending X-box game. Some people live in a dream, afraid to wake up. Some people are locked out of themselves because they're so full of pain. Some people got cast out of their own homes from abuse and misuse. Wherever you are, however it happened, please come home, right now.

Do This Now

"Please come Home, all parts of me, past, present and future me, all dimensions and time-lines of me, loved and unloved parts of me, to the Absolute Highest Truth THAT I AM, right NOW. Thank you"

(We always say Thank you after a request, remember. It means then that it's done, and doesn't leave the request hanging open unanswered. Thank you.)

And we breathe it in again, and FEEL. Stay there.

Base chakras rock. Your 'lower self,' 'shadow self,' 'ego self,' is all necessary; it's good stuff. See what happens when you love and include it, not demean and reject it. Doing so will TOTALLY transform your earthly experience by switching the light on to all that you are. The mystery is hidden in the darkest, most avoided places. Go, look there, and you will find your magnificent self. You are waiting, for you to find you!

Let yourself be made whole again. Let the time-lines merge back to the union of timelessness. Let the strands of your DNA be wrapped into a single cord upon the Lute of the Absolute. Let your senses be woven back into the fabric of True-sense, and embroiled in the ebb and flow dance of the divine. Let your lost identity find its way back to the basket maker. Let your car be parked, your search be benched and your devoted heart find rest in such peace as was never imagined.

There's no home-work now. The work is done, and you are home.

And yet, because this is the wheel of life you're on, and it never stops turning, like the planet never stops spinning and the galaxy never stops swirling, you will go back to step 1 and breathe and receive, and your awakening senses will feel another little cherub of your spirit, out of place and lost in the wilderness of the world. So, you will decide whether to go reclaim it or not. And, if you love yourself enough, you will. And you'll find him or her, your 'little parts of Me' and shower them in acknowledgment for their weary pains, and bathe all over again in forgiveness balm and love medicine. This wheel of your fortune will take you round, and round, on the merry-go-round, feeling the ups, and getting the downs, and at any time you can get off. At any time, you can sit still in the hub of 'home.' At any time you can rest in the harbour of home, when you love yourself enough to get out of the storm; it's always there in the centre of you. The lantern is lit to guide you back. The hearth of Source's love for you never burns out.

The 7 Step Wheel

You have now successfully done One rotation of the 7 steps wheel. Is that enough? Are all you problems solved? Probably not; we've begun a process. Would one rotation of the car wheel be enough to get you from A to B? Does your life even stop at point B?

Like the circle of life, everything cycles back to itself and continues again. Many rotations of the wheel make for a journey. If the wheel stopped after one rotation, or if we stopped after one rotation of Steps 1-7, we wouldn't go very far. We would be stuck again. We'd say, 'Nah, that didn't work,' pridefully keeping our misery.

Of course it works! The wheel turned, it turned once, which means that it can turn again, and needs to turn again and again. Like the cycle of breath, breathe in, wait, breathe out, wait, breathe in again... You don't just get one, and that's it. Life happens, and the living, breathing, loving, releasing appreciating and coming home process must continue moment by moment, day in day out.

The practical application must continue, or we come to a standstill and feel lost and stuck again! If this happens, it means that you didn't properly decide in Step 2, and you need to re-address what you didn't fully commit to. Don't let yourself down. Don't forget. Ultimately you have no one else to blame or make accountable for your happiness. It's your journey, your soul, your purpose being fulfilled; for your human experience to be meaningful and worthwhile. We can throw you a rope, but if you let go of the rope half way through being rescued, then all we can do is throw the rope again. It's up to you to catch it. Catch the lifeline.

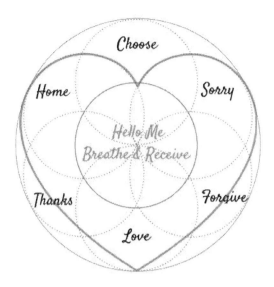

Now that You've taken the 7 steps in this book, you can do anything.

Whatever comes your way next in life, start at the beginning. Do Step 1 - breathe and receive, Always Step 1 first!

There are no shortcuts. This is the short cut! Instead of doing the treadmill of mundane life, and slavery to a system of thinking that doesn't serve you, you could hop on this, and use it as a vehicle to move yourself around. If you have a spoke missing from your wheel, it won't turn smoothly. To keep your life moving and flowing and staying in the NOW, all of these steps are vital for your health, wealth, relationships, clarity, consciousness and Joy. You are at the hub of your life, it all comes back to you. For your Me to be vital, you need to be vital to yourself, in your life. Simple!

When we are close to a breakthrough, the tendency is to turn back. The energy feels too strong — it pushes our buttons, we go into resistance, and want to run. The door to a different world is open to us, but we can stare at the light and tell ourselves, it's not for us. We already have enough light, we don't need what this light is offering us.

We can become very comfortable living in the shadows. Commit. Choose to love yourself enough to never, ever give up.

This will help you to remember.

Go get a brand new cleaning cloth, we're going to write on it so bear that in mind when choosing it. Write the following:

Breathe and Receive - Hello, Me

I now choose to love you enough to end your pain and suffering.

I'm sorry, me

Please forgive me, me

I Love you, me

Thank you, well done, me

Please come home to the truth me,

Thank you.

One wipe is not enough to clean your windows, or the windscreen of your mind. As you would take a cloth, move it in a circular cleaning motion, round and round. Keep moving the cloth in cleaning cycles until the perception is clear, and you can see what's true. When your windscreen is clean you can see the way forward. When it's dirty you grind to a halt. Take out the cloth. Keep it in your pocket. You can use it anywhere.

"There's no place like Home," says Dorothy, as she clicks her heels and commands her way back to where she belongs. (The Wizard of Oz - film 1939) Home is where you'll awaken, and live happily ever after.

Loving Reminder

- STEP 7 -

I LOVE MYSELF ENOUGH TO COME BACK HOME TO ME

❖ I am not separate or alone, but One with my Creator Source.

❖ I love myself enough to return to my Source-self and realise myself.

❖ I am at home in me, I belong in my body, on this earth, right now.

❖ I am at rest in Source.

❖ I complete the cycle when I return home.

❖ I acknowledge my completion with a "well done, me"

❖ Home never leaves me, it's always there.

❖ I hear Home calling me back when I forget, by listening to my feelings.

❖ When I am at home in me, I am in Peace. There's no room for disharmony.

❖ Peace and harmony is my ultimate Truth. Anything else just isn't true.

❖ Truth feels good. Truth is my North.

❖ I found my me, and can continue to keep finding myself within.

❖ Everything I'm looking for is inside of me.

True Stories

"This technique helped me to turn the lens and vision inward in a very real way. We can often speak of self-love and self-acceptance in really abstract ways, but this gets to the matter and has you sensing, feeling, toning and voicing the essence of self-love within. For me, empathising with and holding my inner child was a revelation. I never realised how much pain this part of me carried until this work. I have felt a sense of deep acceptance and homecoming from using this technique. Like I've been seen and heard fully, completely, and wholeheartedly for the first time ever. The joy of it was, that the person doing the deepest listening, embracing and accepting was myself! I feel more confident in just being myself, more able to trust and go with my inner voice and what it's telling me, more able to give myself the validation I need.

It taught me that I need to be held and to be given space that has been prepared lovingly and skilfully by another. I never really appreciated the coaching process as deeply as I did after this work.

"I love you, me" is life-affirming, deeply inspiring and has a sense of home coming about it as you get to release contractions in your energy and expand into a greater sense of being. Without doubt I think self-love is the single most important factor that this dimension, plane of existence, reality and world needs, because it is a force that allows us to experience unification internally, that then gets mirrored externally in every interaction we have.

As I pondered what it would mean if everyone loved themselves this way, for humanity to be unified within themselves and extend this unification to everyone and everything, it made me smile a huge smile. There is no language to describe that, just a warm rush of feeling."

—Tash Mitch - life coach, energy alchemist & author

"The 'I Love You Me' technique has been a powerful process for me. This transformational practice has been a great reminder to come home to the truth of who I am. It's funny because although I teach and guide others in their life and business, I still need support and reminding to home back home to me in my own life. We can all get lost in our own crap sometimes!

Every time I say 'Hello me', my body relaxes. That little part inside of me loves to be acknowledged. And when I welcome myself home, I find peace. Everything that I was looking for or longing for is finally met, when I come back home to me.

I use Tara's I Love You Me process whenever I have fallen out of flow or lost my balance. I find 'I Love You Me' especially useful when I am emotionally triggered. It's so easy to be seduced into focusing on the outside world as the source of pain. The answers and healing for my pain always lie within.

Thank you Tara for being there and for seeing the truth of who I am. Your 1:1 VIP sessions and your I Love You Me process has had a deep impact on my life and my Soul's journey. What an incredible gift you have. Your love, your wisdom and mentorship has been invaluable to me, my life and my business.

—Lara Waldman, Author of 'Money Manifestation Mastery'

The End Meets the Beginning

DANCING ALL THE STEPS TOGETHER

When pain, disharmony, or any situation of suffering or feeling stuck occurs, stop and get present with where you are right now.

Step 1 ~ I'm willing to love myself enough to connect with me.

Take a breath and say "hello, me."

Continue to Breathe and receive with a soft open mouth for a few breaths and start to return all your senses back to you.

(Touch, inner-sight, inner-listening, empathy, taste and sense.)

Step 2 ~ Am I willing to love myself enough to transform this situation/feeling and stop suffering?

If so, a) choose to own your power and take it back off whomever you've given it to. b) Choose to take responsibility for how you feel right now. c) Choose to take care of yourself independently (which includes asking for the right people or The How Genie for help). d) Organise and set your priority need or want, and e) Dedicate yourself to doing so.

If not, then wait till it gets worse, and maybe come back later.

Step 3 ~ Am I willing to be the one to acknowledge beautifully the pain that I'm feeling, for it can't, and won't change until I do?

Say out loud, I'm sorry me, I'm sorry you're _____ (name the situation — stuck, in pain, lost etc) me, and feeling (angry, sad, confused etc) _____. (Breathe)

Step 4 ~ Am I willing to love myself enough to once and for all release my pain and addiction to suffering?

Please forgive me, me (i.e., please be willing to release all this now, me), that I think it's true that _____ (name the person) did or didn't _____, and _____, and _____, and caused you to feel_____, and _____, and _____. (Breathe)

Step 5 ~ Am I now willing to love myself enough to love every part of me, unconditionally?

I love you, me, that feels all that _____ and believes all that_____. (Breathe)

Step 6 ~ Am I willing to bathe myself in appreciation and gratitude for my existence?

Thank you, me. (Breathe)

Step 7 ~ Am I willing to love myself enough to come home and self realise?

Please come home now, _____ (hurt, angry, lost, stuck, sad etc) Me; back to the truth. I need you. I want you. I love you. Thank you. Well done, me." (Breathe)

And now ask all the other directions to release from you too, by saying,

"I'm sorry all people and directions (name them if you need or want to) involved in my pain. I'm sorry I let you hurt me and cause me to be helpless in this situation now. I'm sorry you think you can have my power. I'm sorry that you're probably also hurting and suffering now too." (Breathe)

"Please forgive me all directions and people involved, past present and future. Please forgive me that you thought you could have my power, that I was your victim and that you could this to me. Please forgive me that in my innocence or ignorance I let you do that to me. Please forgive me that I now choose to reclaim my power and that you can no longer have it." (Breathe)

"I love you, all people and aspects of this situation, seen and unseen." (Breathe)

"Thank you for releasing me and returning to source all that we no longer need, for the highest good of all, now." (Breathe)

"Please come home, back to the truth, right now, Thank you."

Breathe and Receive.

Any stubborn areas, go back and attend to it more thoroughly.

Bring your attention back to yourself. Seal the space with "I love you, me, well done, me, thank you, me."

And that's it!

Hopefully you followed the chapters with your workbook, and did some soul gardening as we went along. In which case, you've got this now.

If you haven't, because like me, you just want to get through all the steps and get to the end of the book quickly, or you couldn't be bothered, I recommend you go to the workbook now and do the exercises. But that's up to you, if you love yourself enough to do the homework. ☺

If you've enjoyed reading this book and learning how to love yourself, why not share it! Who do you know who needs to love themselves some more?

Go to www.iloveyoume.co.uk

~ Thank you!

Epilogue

HOW DOES ALL THIS CHANGE THE WORLD?

Has your world changed as result of reading this book? You've probably had quite a few revelations, even the most seasoned of spiritual people do. I wrote this book, and reading it still reminds me when I forget! The 7 steps are my daily bread and still they cause me to evolve. The learning never stops and the potential to grow is infinite. By the impact that this has had on you, thus far, how *do you think* self love can change the world?

When you feel light, free, happy, in love, what are you be capable of? When you discover who you are by cleaning off all that dust and debris, the concrete from your Buddha, don't you want to show it to the world? Don't you just want to shout out your new revelations from the roof tops, or paint about it, write about it, or sing about it? When you are lit, you are compelled to share it. When you're strong independently, you want to collaborate. The world needs your message. It needs your joy!

Imagine an ocean, made of billions and billions of tiny drops. Each one doesn't know its value. It can't see itself. It's a bit too dark to see clearly. What happens when your drop lights up? When your drop feels a powerful feeling like love or appreciation, or peace, or happiness? Those who want what you've got will flock to you. Those who don't, won't. They will leave. You will lead others simply by being an example; your authentic self. Your story of how you got there is a legacy for others to learn from. Your light shows the way and shows others their potential. It gives permission to shine without fear or without reprisal.

How many drops of light would it take to light up the ocean?

How many singers in a choir does it take to pull the others into harmony?

How many people in peace does it take to spread it to a room full of people?

How many people in love does it take to love-up a crowd?

If all life is basically energy, expressed through frequencies, acting according to certain laws of Creation, what is your frequency? What tune are you playing? Your harmonic resonance can change a whole orchestra. Your vibration creates ripples.

When you are in peace, your actions come from a place of peace. When you are happy, your actions inspire happiness and create joy. When you feel beautiful, you bring beauty to the world. When you are in love, you sow seeds of love where ever you go. The inner reality is the only reality where you can effect sustainable, and lasting change that's based on truth. All else is good ideas, great intentions and actions taken in unconsciousness and misalignment.

If you thought you were doing your healing only for your own sake, nope. You are doing far more than you could even imagine, for the sake of your ancestors and all of humanity. You are tidying up the mess of history! You are becoming conscious of what our ancestors before us had not yet learned. You are literally a hero!

You probably don't feel like one, but if you think about it, for all that you've come through, just to still be here, right now, reading this page... for all that you've inherited, and have carried throughout your life so far... for all the love, effort, good intention, trials and errors that you have made, to survive and get through it - WELL DONE! You are a blessed hero my friend, and I LOVE YOU! I know what you have come though.

This book was written specifically for you, so that you are acknowledged, so that you recognise and validate yourself. To see a bigger picture of 'Why' you feel the way you do, and to offer you a way out. You are the solution.

Your joy and peace never left you.

Your healthy, well body never left you.

Everything fails and fades through lack of presence; your presence. Be Present!

Love, Tara

Next Steps

Watch The 7 Steps To Transformational Self-Love In Action

ENJOY A 1:1 LEARNING EXPERIENCE WITH TARA LOVE PERRY IN THIS ELEGANT, EASY TO DIGEST E-COURSE.

In Your E-Course Bundle You Will Receive:

- *A warm welcome video*

- *Steps 1-7 Videos - Each Step beautifully outlined and demonstrated over 7 videos*

- *The Method video - Tips and techniques for how to implement this simple method successfully*

- *The Practice Video - How to use "I love you, me" with other people, and in everyday life situations with easy and flow.*

- *The Next Steps Video - Where do you go from here? Practice the 7 steps with others like yourself at Live events with Tara, and feel the healing benefits as she guides you through your inner world. Also, find out how would you bring this method to your current work or area of passion to help others?*

- *A workbook PDF*

If, like me, you're the sort of person who needs to see something in action so that you fully understand it, then this concise video e-course will be invaluable to you.
It's informative to watch and relaxing to listen to - filmed in a tranquil Sri Lankan retreat with the soothing sounds of the rainforest in the background - you are gently and effortlessly guided through the fundamental process. It couldn't be simpler, and the next best thing to a live event!

If you'd like to find out more, please visit this link www.iloveyoume.co.uk/e-course.html

Thank You

For Purchasing This Book!

17% of the profits from your purchase go to the 'Empower Bricks' Foundation.

From there we directly fund ALALA, a charity that builds orphanages for and helps to feed orphans of natural disasters and war. A portion also goes to Catalytic Wellbeing, a foundation dedicated to creating ethical, long-term sustainable and biodiverse futures with land-based and community projects.

Thank you for helping to make this possible.

Winged Heart Logo Copyright 2017 Tara Love Perry

ALALA is a registered charity in England and Wales, number: 1140248
If you want to contact us Phone/fax: +44/0 1273 677178 or +44/0 7739 728433 Email: info@alala.org.uk

Made in the USA
Monee, IL
11 December 2020